Blogging in One Hour FOR LAWYERS

ERNIE SVENSON

LawPracticeManagementSection

MARKETING • MANAGEMENT • TECHNOLOGY • FINANCE

Commitment to Quality: The Law Practice Management Section is committed to quality in our publications. Our authors are experienced practitioners in their fields. Prior to publication, the contents of all our books are rigorously reviewed by experts to ensure the highest quality product and presentation. Because we are committed to serving our readers' needs, we welcome your feedback on how we can improve future editions of this book.

Cover design by RIPE Creative, Inc.

Nothing contained in this book is to be considered as the rendering of legal advice for specific cases, and readers are responsible for obtaining such advice from their own legal counsel. This book and any forms and agreements herein are intended for educational and informational purposes only.

The products and services mentioned in this publication are under or may be under trademark or service mark protection. Product and service names and terms are used throughout only in an editorial fashion, to the benefit of the product manufacturer or service provider, with no intention of infringement. Use of a product or service name or term in this publication should not be regarded as affecting the validity of any trademark or service mark.

The Law Practice Management Section, American Bar Association, offers an educational program for lawyers in practice. Books and other materials are published in furtherance of that program. Authors and editors of publications may express their own legal interpretations and opinions, which are not necessarily those of either the American Bar Association or the Law Practice Management Section unless adopted pursuant to the bylaws of the Association. The opinions expressed do not reflect in any way a position of the Section or the American Bar Association.

© 2012 American Bar Association. All rights reserved.

Printed in the United States of America

15 14 13 12   5 4 3 2 1

Library of Congress Cataloging-in-Publication Data

Svenson, Ernie.
    Blogging in one hour for lawyers / Ernie Svenson.
        p. cm.
    Includes bibliographical references and index.
    ISBN 978-1-61438-522-6 (alk. paper)
    1. Lawyers—United States—Blogs. 2. Law firms—United States—Blogs. 3. Blogs—Economic aspects.
4. Law firms—Internet marketing. 5. Lawyers—United States—Handbooks, manuals, etc. I. Title.
    KF320.I57S88   2012
    006.7'5202434—dc23

                                                        2012038215

Discounts are available for books ordered in bulk. Special consideration is given to state bars, CLE programs, and other bar-related organizations. Inquire at Book Publishing, American Bar Association, 321 N. Clark Street, Chicago, Illinois 60654.

www.ShopABA.org

Contents

About the Author

Ernie Svenson practiced commercial litigation for 26 years, first with a mid-sized New Orleans law firm, and then for six years as a solo practitioner. He's now a full-time speaker on tech-related topics.

He started his first blog—ernietheattorney.net—in 2002. It was one of five law-related blogs at the time, and it was chosen as an ABA Top 100 Blog two years in a row. Shortly after, he created PDFforLawyers.com, a blog to help lawyers learn to make better use of PDF files in their practice. He started a CLE company (paperlesschase.com) that helps lawyers develop a paperless law practice, and, more recently, he co-founded SocialSuits.co, a website devoted to the effects of social media on lawsuits and the lawyers who try them.

Ernie believes the practice of law is largely an information-processing business, and he strives to help lawyers process their information better. He makes extensive use of social media tools (e.g., LinkedIn, Twitter, and Facebook) to promote his ideas. When he isn't blogging, tweeting, or surfing the web, he likes to play his guitar for captive audiences (who usually escape quickly as soon as he starts singing).

To find out more about him, just Google "ernie attorney."

Acknowledgments

Thanks to Denise Constantine, Lindsay Dawson, and Laura Bolesta of the American Bar Association for proposing the book, managing the production, and providing expert guidance. Thanks to Jennifer Ator and Carole Levitt for their peer review and helpful suggestions. Thanks as well to Graham da Ponte who polished my gangly prose, making it simple and easy to understand.

Thanks to those who helped me start my first blog, and get it noticed: Buzz Bruggeman, Dave Winer, Robert Scoble, Jenny Levine, David Weinberger, Denise Howell, Rick Klau, Marty Schwimmer, Walter Olsen, Glenn Reynolds, Shel Israel, Dan Gilmor, Dennis Kennedy, Jim Calloway, and Tom Mighell.

Thanks to the folks who helped shaped this book: Jeff Richardson, Molly DiBianca, David Sparks, Jordan Furlong, Kevin O'Keefe, and Jeff Lantz.

Most of all, thanks to the hundreds of wonderful people I've met during the past 10 years, all because one day I started a blog and somehow managed to keep it going.

Introduction

Blogs Are Powerful Tools

More than 100 million people have created blogs, gaining immediate access to a worldwide audience. Twenty years ago, only large companies could afford to engage on such a global scale. Today, blogs are available to anyone at little or no cost.

Lawyers have the same ability to take advantage of blogs as anyone else. The question for many lawyers pondering a jump into the blogosphere is, will it be worth it?

For me, it's been well worth it. Having two law-related blogs raised my web profile, which led to more clients, more referrals from other lawyers, more requests for media interviews, and a host of other valuable opportunities. And my experience is far from unusual.

Here's what other longtime law bloggers say about their experiences:

- "As a promotional tool, the weblog has been a huge success. I've had a lot of press attention about my legal work that I wouldn't have had without it."—Evan Schaeffer, a lawyer in Alton, Illinois, who created "Beyond The Underground"

- "It is a real kick to go to some small town in rural Oklahoma and have someone say 'I read your blog all of the time.' But I've also gotten e-mail from as far away as the Attorney General's Office of Guam thanking me for a post."—Jim Calloway, Oklahoma lawyer who created "Jim Calloway's Law Practice Tips"

A Small Law Blog Can Do Great Things

When the U.S. Supreme Court released its decision upholding the Affordable Care Act, SCOTUSblog was ready with a quick legal analysis. This was a natural topic for Tom Goldstein and Amy Howe, the two lawyers who run the site, because they practice almost exclusively before the Supreme Court.

Blogs have been around for more than 10 years, and lots of lawyers have them; it's not surprising that a niche blog was ready to comment quickly on the Supreme Court opinion. What's interesting is that the mainstream press was waiting for SCOTUSblog to comment as eagerly as it was waiting for the opinion itself. Within minutes of the opinion's release, *The Atlantic* magazine's website ran a short article under the headline: "The Health Care Decision, Explained in 1 Paragraph on SCOTUSblog."

Meanwhile, the broadcast news stations CNN and Fox initially misreported that the Court had struck down the healthcare law, setting off a chain reaction of misinformation that propagated quickly via social media. The next day, *The Wall Street Journal* ran a short article about the media confusion, ending with praise for one law blog:

> "A small Supreme Court blog normally read only by lawyers and other hard-core law enthusiasts, SCOTUSblog, was the go-to place for many Washington insiders to learn of the decision. The blog posted the decision correctly at 10:07 a.m."

These days, no one can deny the power of blogs. Their power is, of course, directly proportional to the power of the Internet itself. In a recent House of Delegates resolution, the American Bar Association observed that, ". . . the Internet, and other forms of electronic communication are now among the most powerful media for getting information to the public. . . ." The resolution doesn't reference blogs specifically, but you can be sure that the ABA Standing Committee was aware of blogs' growing role in society.

So, what does it take to start and maintain a law blog? You don't need much money, simply a willingness to learn to use the tools properly, which is what this book is about. Presumably you're willing or you wouldn't be reading this book. In the pages that follow, you'll find out how to set up a basic blog, how to craft compelling content, and how to get optimal attention from the right audience.

Obviously, this book doesn't contain everything you need to know about law-related blogging. That's why I set up a blog called <u>onehrblog.</u> <u>com</u>, so the conversation can continue on the Internet, which is the hometown to every blog—including the one you are about to set up.

The Agenda

- **Lesson 1: Basic Questions.** This lesson explains where blogs came from, why you should establish one, and what you should consider before you do, including ethical issues related to blogging.

- **Lesson 2: Examining the Blog Anatomy.** The components of a blog and the elements of a blog post are in this lesson.

- **Lesson 3: Selecting Your Blog Tools.** You need a unique domain name, a web host, and blog software. Many choices are available, but I focus on three: one that's free, one that's popular, and one that's feature-rich and easy to set up.

- **Lesson 4: Setting Up Your Blog.** I explain step by step how to set up a blog and the best options to choose. The lesson focuses on TypePad hosting and software, but the information and options apply to whatever blog software you choose.

- **Lesson 5: Designing Your Blog.** You'll want to tweak the design of your blog, and select the right layout and colors. I show you how to make those choices.

- **Lesson 6: Posting to Your Blog.** Here you'll learn how to create, edit, and format a blog post, and how to create proper hyperlinks. Also included are the use of multimedia content, such as images and movies, and social media tools, such as Facebook and Twitter.

- **Lesson 7: Getting Attention and Monitoring It.** Once you start a blog, you'll want to learn how to build an audience and keep it growing. I also explain how to measure your blog's traffic and how to craft posts that raise your blog's profile with search engines.

- **Lesson 8: Gathering Information.** Coming up with material to write about isn't hard if you know the secrets of RSS feeds and RSS readers. The information you need is available for free, and I'll show you which tools you need to gather it efficiently.

- **Final Thoughts.** What are the ethical perils in blogging, and how can you best avoid them? And what is my best tip for building a successful blog? That's what I cover here.

- **Appendix.** I briefly provide three resources that will help a new blogger get started:
  - ▸ Recommended Legal Blogs
  - ▸ Recommended Reading
  - ▸ Checklist for New Bloggers

As you can see, there's a lot of information to cover. Let's get right to it, starting with the preliminary things you should ponder carefully before committing to starting a blog.

Basic Questions

A few questions may persist, ones you want answered before you start setting up a blog. Our first section will deal with those concerns.

Why the Goofy Name?

A blog is a website, but it's a more evolved type of website. The word *blog* is short for *weblog,* a name that makes sense once you understand how blogs evolved. Websites are what most people are used to, and they've dominated the Internet for a long time (and probably still do). They're great for posting content that doesn't change much, but they're not great for content that evolves or changes frequently.

The blog developed to allow posts with new information to appear at the top of a page, pushing older content down. Since a journal is a form of *log* (as in a ship captain's log), the new tool was called a *web log*, then shortened to *weblog*, and finally to *blog*.

Denise Howell (an early law blogger with a site called Bag and Baggage at bagandbaggage.com) further modified the term to *blawg*, to connote a blog written by a lawyer, or one that covers a legal topic.

Why Should You Blog?

Google yourself. Yes, right now, go to your computer and search Google for your name and examine the results. If you have a common name, add *lawyer* to the search. Or add your hometown or your law firm name. Keep revising your search results until you have a sense of how "findable" you are, and once found, what the results show.

Maybe you're findable, but what shows up is uninteresting. Worse, you're not findable at all. If you have a website and it's not showing up easily, then you are paying for something that doesn't work well.

Sure there are companies out there that promise to give you "a web presence" and then charge you a monthly fee to maintain it. Odds are you're being overcharged, and the results are paltry. If you want a strong web presence, you can have it. It won't cost much—almost certainly less than what many of those companies are charging—but it will take an investment of some time.

Here's the thing: you want to have as much control over what people learn about you on the web as you can. Having that control is not hard, it just takes consistent effort and the right tool. A blog is the best tool for this job.

Many small businesses have no website at all. The same is true for many solo and small-firm lawyers. If you don't have a web presence, then you have forsaken any chance to get business from people who are trying to find a lawyer online. Reporters looking for a legal expert to comment on a specialized topic that you are versed in won't call you. They can't easily find you.

You need a website. And you need to have full control over it, so you can update it and adjust it to do the best job possible to promote yourself and your practice. A blog is the best choice. It can do everything a website can do, and more.

If you're in a mid-sized to large firm, you probably already have a website. Do you have a blog? You can get a professional-looking one set up and designed for around $3,500. If you're in a small firm, or if you have a solo practice, you can get a blog set up for under $500. The annual cost of keeping a blog running is generally around $200.

For this investment, which includes the time to update the blog and keep the content fresh, you will become much more findable. And you will have fine-grained control over what people find when they search for you. Will it result in new business? Probably, if you're sincere and thoughtful and if you put out useful information. If you help other bloggers and show that you genuinely care about people and about your profession, you will get business.

Blogging makes you findable, but how people perceive you when they find you is even more important. You want them to know you care about people and about your profession. You want to be trusted, and a blog gives you a platform on which to build readers' trust.

You shouldn't blog just so you show up more frequently in Google search results. You should blog so you can help people understand you better, and if you do, you'll find tremendous rewards. You'll meet new people, and some of the people you already know will learn more about you.

What Ethics Rules Apply?

Obviously, you can't use your blog to make false or misleading statements (ABA Model Rule 7.1). Be mindful that something you post today may turn out to be wrong tomorrow, and therefore arguably misleading or false. Disclaimers can help address this issue. Draft a short statement that information on your site was believed to be accurate at the time it was written, and that readers should be careful about relying on any online information. Of course, if you become aware that a post is no longer accurate, you should take it down or edit it to make it accurate. Most blog posts are automatically date- and time-stamped, which helps readers assess the timeliness of the information, but it's still a good idea to update posts when you learn that they've become so outdated that they could be misleading.

ABA Formal Opinion 10-457 cautions that information on the website is considered a communication about the lawyer or the lawyer's services under Model Rule 7.1 and therefore must not be false or misleading. Rule 7.2 of the ABA Model Rules addresses what lawyers must do when they advertise. Research your local rules regarding advertising and professional promotion to find out what restrictions might apply and how you must comply.

If you're writing a blog that simply puts out general information about legal topics, it's unlikely you'll be deemed to be engaged in advertising. To be safe, however, get a sense of your jurisdiction's rules about creating websites and other online content. Call your bar association and find out who is most knowledgeable about these issues and talk to that person. Get in touch with law bloggers in your jurisdiction; ask them what advice they can offer. In short, do the basic research.

What Will Be the Focus of Your Blog?

You probably learned in grade school that every essay should begin with a theme sentence. Having a guiding theme is good for blogs as well as essays.

Today there are thousands of law-related blogs. You can go to Justia. com and survey the vast array, and you probably should, so you can see what the spectrum is and whether your idea for a blog already exists. Having a strong focus is critical for making your blog stand out from the mass and for attracting a loyal audience. Well-thought-out answers to the following questions will help you find your focus.

- Who is your ideal audience and what are your goals in reaching that audience? If you want to establish yourself as an expert in a special area of law so that you get invited to speak to industry groups, determine who makes those kinds of decisions and what kind of information appeals to them.
- Who might come across your blog whom you would also appreciate having as a reader? Potential clients might read your blog. Journalists looking for an expert to interview might stumble across your blog, and other bloggers will undoubtedly find it, too.
- What kinds of issues and topics do you enjoy writing about?
- Is there some issue that's particularly hot and likely to remain so? And do you have expertise in that area?
- Are there already law blogs that cover the hot issues you want to talk about? If so, can you bring out something they're not addressing to differentiate your blog?
- Will your blog have a different design or writing style than other law-related blogs on the topics you want to address? Focus isn't only about picking a narrow set of topics. Your approach can be part of your focus, too. If your "competition" is erudite and comprehensive, you can be witty and breezy.

Answering these questions will help you determine the main theme of your blog. It's better to work through them now than to introduce a major theme shift after you've been blogging and built up an audience.

How Long Will Typical Posts Be?

Some lawyers write lengthy posts that go into great detail about a topic. Others, like Howard Bashman's "How Appealing" blog (howappealing.law. com), employ short blurbs that quickly highlight breaking news, followed by a link to an original source. Short posts are easier to write, but you have to write more of them and do so consistently, or your audience will find someone else who does. An audience will be more willing to accept less frequent posts when those posts that finally arrive are worth the wait—which means they take longer to write.

A corollary to the question about the length of posts is how much time you have to create content. If you don't have much time, but can find small chunks of time each day, then short posts about breaking news in a niche area that you already pay attention to make sense. If you have time sporadically, then longer posts that show you've thought deeply about an issue are probably more suitable.

Decide what the typical length of your posts will be before you start posting anything, and then stick to that approach.

Who Will Create Posts?

In a big law firm, there are lots of lawyers who could write for a firm blog. If you have several lawyers in your firm, maybe you will have help in creating posts. If you have the luxury of choosing who will contribute to your law blog, you should determine the workflow. For example, one person could assign topics, while another group is tasked with writing.

In the beginning, it's probably best not to have too many people involved. You want your blog to have a unique voice, and that's harder with multiple writers. However, if the style of the blog is sober analysis, a variety of voices may work.

One thing that may not work well is delegating the task of writing your blog posts to an outsider. There are companies that will ghost-blog for a fee, and the lure of out-sourcing the arduous task of writing may sound appealing. For lawyers, however, there is danger in that lure.

Some states have strict rules about what lawyers can say, and to whom they say it. If you hire someone to write your blog and they unknowingly violate those rules, you won't be absolved of blame; you will be deemed responsible for all content that appears on your website.

The same problem can arise even if you have junior lawyers in your firm writing. If you're not writing the words that appear on your blog, make sure you are closely supervising whoever is and approving all content before it's published to the web (ABA Model Rule 5.1).

What Will the Writing Style Be?

Many law blogs are written in a no-nonsense, objective style. But that's not a requirement. Some very successful law blogs are often sarcastic or irreverent. You should suit your writing style to your topic and your audience. But remember, even for serious topics, there's an opportunity to be creative and take a fresh approach.

Will Images or Multimedia Be Used?

Are you going to stick to straight text with no pictures? Or will you occasionally have images and interesting graphics? Check out Josh Gilliland's "Bow Tie Law Blog" (bowtielaw.wordpress.com). Josh is a great writer, but notice too that his photos help make a dry topic (e-Discovery) much more appealing.

If you do use images, you need to be careful about where you get them. Images can be copyrighted even if they're not accompanied by a notice, so grabbing an image from the Internet or elsewhere can create havoc. Instead, consider using online stock photo companies, such as istockphoto.com or shutterstock.com. When you buy an image from a stock photo company, you get not only an image but also defined rights about how those pictures can be used. In most cases, the costs for image rights for a blog are very affordable.

What Do Other Law Bloggers Advise?

If you know any law bloggers, call them or take them to lunch to get some free advice. Ask them to describe what it was like to get a blog up and running, and if they can share anything that will spare you needless agony. If you don't know what all to ask, here are five questions you can use as a rough template:

- What professional benefits have you had from blogging?
- Were there any unexpected challenges to blogging?
- Looking back to when you started, what goals did you have for your blog?
- Given what you know now, what advice would you give a lawyer who's just beginning to blog?
- If you were going to start over, what three things would you do differently?

You can pose questions like these to law bloggers that you find at the *ABA Journal*'s online Blawg Directory: abajournal.com/blawgs, or at Justia. com. Both sources list hundreds of law-related blogs. If you e-mail a few of the bloggers on those lists you might be surprised at their generosity. Even better, attend the "Beer for Bloggers" event held every year during the ABA TECHSHOW in Chicago.

Consider Guest Posting

You don't necessarily need to have your own blog to get a feel for what it's like to post to one. Several lawyers have started out by posting content to someone else's blog. Some don't even want to have their own blog.

Scout out some blogs that have multiple authors and see if they'd be willing to let you put up some posts. Consider writing one post every week for a couple of weeks to get a sense of whether you will find blogging exhilarating or burdensome. Better to find out before you spend too much time and money setting one up.

Go to Blogger.com (see Lesson 3) and set up a simple blog there for free. Then practice creating posts and formatting them. In particular, practice the important art of creating hyperlinks (see Lesson 6). Don't *publish* the content; just practice *creating* it. That way you can tell the manager of the site for which you're guest blogging that you know how to create and edit posts.

Examining the Blog Anatomy

Let's talk about the components of a blog. And let's also address what makes up a typical blog post.

The Elements of a Blog

What makes a blog a blog? Despite what some might think, it's not a stupid question. Before you start, you should know the components of a typical blog. At this point, you might not have any idea what they are.

Using my "Ernie the Attorney" blog as an example (see Figure 2.1), let's take a look at which elements make it a blog as opposed to a simple website.

To most web surfers, there's no apparent difference between a website and a blog. The main distinction is noted by those who post to weblogs: blogs are easier to update than websites. If you've ever managed a website, you can appreciate the agony of having to update it. Since most of you probably haven't, let's put aside the behind-the-scenes differences for now. Instead, let's focus on the visual components of a typical blog—the stuff readers might notice.

Figure 2.1 Visual Components of a Blog

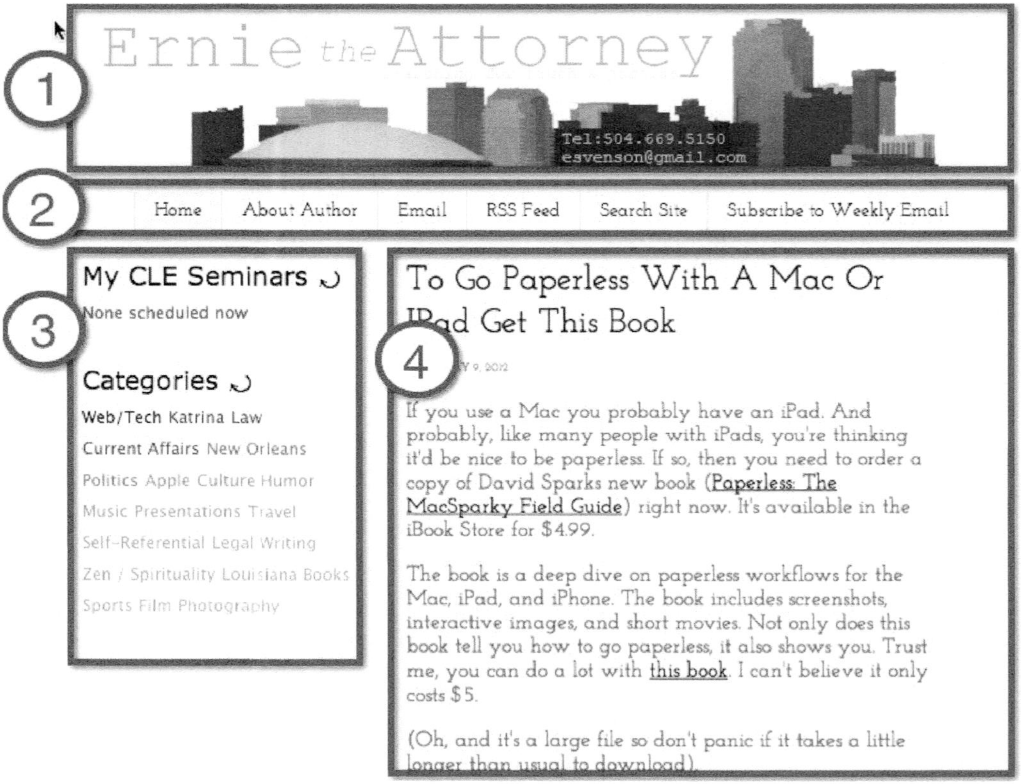

1. **The header.** A horizontal banner runs across the top of every page of the blog. The blog software you use may steer you into using a particular type of header, but you can change the header and use a graphic image if you prefer.

2. **The navigation links.** The blog navigation links typically appear below the header, and those are created automatically (but usually they can be modified).

3. **The sidebar.** Often the sidebar appears along the left-hand side of the page, but it can be set to appear on the right-hand side. Some blogs have sidebars on both sides.

Here's the key thing to know: the sidebar appears on every page of the blog, and it is used to post lists of useful links, or other small bits of information. Basically, everything that's not a blog post goes in a sidebar.

4. **The main section.** This is where the blog posts appear, in chronological order (the most recent post on top, then the next most recent, and so on). You can configure your blog to show a certain number of posts, with the older ones archived automatically. Don't worry—the archived posts are still accessible to people searching on the web (another reason blogs are better than websites).

The Elements of a Blog Post

Every blog post has three main elements: (1) the title, (2) the body, and (3) the footer (see Figure 2.2). (As I've already mentioned, the banner appears at the top of every page.)

Figure 2.2 Elements of a Blog Post

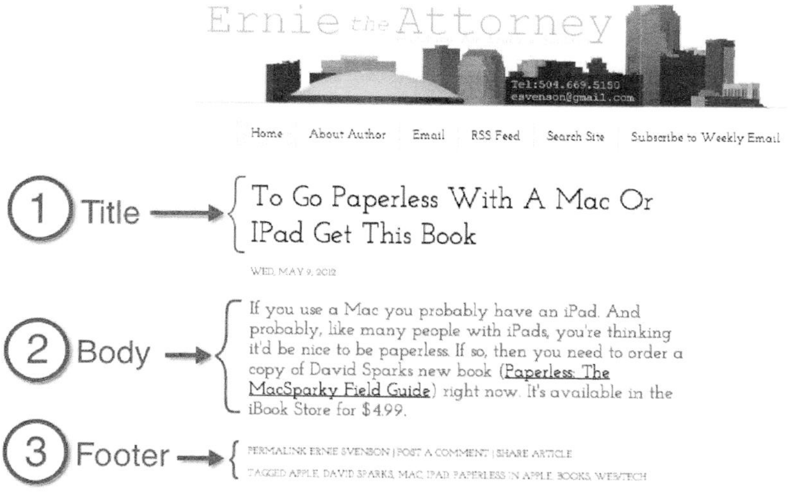

1. The Title

The title is a short description of what the blog post is about, ideally written in a way that is not only informative, but also enticing. Many, if not most, web readers make snap decisions about whether to read a blog post based on the description contained in the title. And because readers who want to alert others to your post will often copy the title as they link to the blog post, the title has a lot of hidden power.

I'll cover how to write compelling headlines later; for now, suffice it to say you want to spend some time thinking about how to describe your blog post. Short, provocative headlines are best.

2. The Body

The body of the post is where you write what you have to say. Obviously. What's not obvious at first is that writing a blog post is more than putting down words. You'll almost certainly include hyperlinks to other information. As a lawyer, you're familiar with the idea of providing sources for your positions; citing to cases and statutory materials is a staple requirement of legal writing. Hyperlinks are used in the same way, except the link has to be to a public source on the Internet.

Hyperlinking is important for lots of reasons, and there is an art to doing it well. For now, just realize it's important; it will help you get more readers, and you'll have to factor it into your writing.

3. The Footer

The footer is where additional information appears. Typically, such information includes the name of the post author, followed by some other tidbits. What appears in the footer is configurable; some of the information is created automatically for each post. For example, the "permalink" is an active hyperlink, created automatically, allowing a reader to permanently link to the post in a way that will pull it up even after it's been archived.

The words *post a comment* (see Figure 2.2) form a hyperlink (automatically created) that pulls up a dialogue box so that readers can leave comments on the post. You don't have to allow comments, and many bloggers don't. We'll talk about comments in more detail in Lesson 6.

Note also in the footer area of Figure 2.2 the word *tagged* followed by *Apple, David Sparks, Mac, iPad, Paperless.* These are keywords that help search engines identify topics by which the post can be grouped. You have to decide which keywords to use for each post; they don't get created automatically.

Finally, you see the words *Apple, Books, Web/Tech.* These are categories within which the post is grouped, and here again, you have to choose them for each post. In the footer area, these category words are live hyperlinks: clicking on one will pull up all blog posts grouped under that category. Categories will be covered in Lesson 6 as well.

Selecting Your Blog Tools

The key blogging tools are: a domain name, a web host, and blogging software. Because blogging is now a mature business, there are many choices among those tools. In fact, the number of choices can be overwhelming. The "right" choice depends on factors such as:

- Are you comfortable with technology, especially if it's web-based?
- If not, are you willing to pay a little bit more for assistance with setup and design?
- Are you part of a mid-sized or large firm that has a budget to pay for setup and design?
- Are you just setting up a stand-alone blog, or are you looking to integrate it into your existing website?

For mid-sized firms or larger, I'd recommend going with one of the leading companies that specializes in legal blogs. Expect to pay about $3,500 for basic setup and design. If you want a super sleek design, the cost will quickly rise from there.

The first company to specialize in helping lawyers and law firms create blogs was LexBlog (lexblog.com), which now has more than 1,000 law blogs in its portfolio. Esquire Interactive (esquireinteractive.com) also specializes in helping lawyers set up blogs. Both companies use WordPress software, the leading software for blogging.

WordPress is free, but you have to install it on a web host site (or pay someone to do that), and the hosting is what you pay for. If you're web-savvy, or know and can pay someone who is, then you should definitely opt for WordPress software. We'll cover the benefits of WordPress later.

But what if you're not web-savvy, or just want a simple tool that anyone can set up? Most of you probably fit in that camp. I'm going to review several options in the pages that follow, but if you're not tech-savvy and don't have access to someone who is, here's my suggestion: get a domain name at Hover.com ($15 per year), or GoDaddy.com (slightly cheaper), and then use the blogging software and hosting provided by TypePad.com ($10 per month). Anyone can set up a blog with those two options (especially since we're going to walk through the setup using those tools as examples). The cost is affordable, too. If you want to pay TypePad to do the setup (including the domain connection) and help with the design, it'll cost $350. So, at most, you'd spend that plus $125 per year for your blog.

But no matter what blogging software you use, or where you host your blog, you should begin by getting a unique domain name. So, let's talk about that first.

Domain Name: What It Is, Why You Need One

A domain is an address for a website or blog, and it's like a street address. Let's say your clients want to find your law firm building. If they have your street address, they can punch it into their car's GPS system and it will guide them directly to your building. Likewise, a domain name will guide anyone's web browser to your website, which is hosted by a company you pay a monthly fee (see Figure 3.1).

Figure 3.1 A Domain Points to the Web Host Location

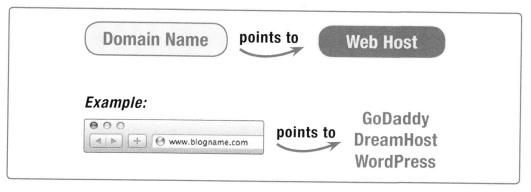

Unlike your office address, however, you get to choose a phrase or word string to serve as your web address, as long as that phrase or word string is not already claimed.

A website's address includes the domain name, which appears in the title bar of your browser when you're on the site. (If your site has several pages, the web address of each page also includes page-specific information.) One way to get to a known site is to enter the address into the address field of the browser and hit Return. You can also enter keywords and phrases into a search engine and click on the site's link in the resulting list. Either way you get there, that address is displayed on the title bar of the website's home page.

In Figure 3.2, you see the address for my blog is displayed as <u>www.</u> <u>ernietheattorney.net</u>.

Figure 3.2 Browser Displays Website Address

My blog's domain is ernietheattorney.net. I would have preferred that it end in *.com*, but the domain ernietheattorney.com was already taken. Odds are some of the obvious choices for your blog will be taken as well. Don't despair. You can still find good domain names that will work.

Here are things to keep in mind when choosing a domain name:

- It should be as short as possible.
- It should be easy to remember, so people can find your site easily.
- It should include some words or a phrase contained within the name of your blog name.
- It can be a clever play on words, or even funny—whatever helps people remember it.
- It can include your name (e.g., ernietheattorney, which worked for me).

If you're having trouble coming up with a domain name, there are online sites such as bustaname.com that can help you brainstorm the process.

Ethics Alert: you shouldn't use *.org* in your domain name if you're not a non-profit organization. And you probably shouldn't pick a domain name like "Bestlawyer.com," lest you be deemed to be making improper claims under your state's lawyer ethics rules.

Registering Your Domain Name

The act of buying your domain name from a registrar is called *domain registration*. Actually, you're not really buying the domain; you're renting it. When you find an available domain, you'll be given the option of holding it for a certain period of time—e.g., one year, five years, etc. At the end of the term, you'll be given the option to renew; if you don't, the name will revert to the open market.

Here are several well-known domain registration services:

- **Network Solutions** (networksolutions.com): The first big-name registrar is also probably the most expensive. Domain names start at $34.99 per year as of this writing.

- **Go Daddy** (godaddy.com): Known for its provocative Superbowl ads, Go Daddy is more of a discount house. It also provides blog hosting, so you might opt to register here if you want an all-in-one solution for domain hosting and web hosting (which will be discussed below). Domain names go for $11.99 per year.

- **Hover** (hover.com): This domain registrar is gaining popularity because its interface is uncluttered, and there are no annoying efforts to constantly up-sell you to services you likely don't want. Also, the telephone support is incredible. However, unlike Go Daddy, it doesn't offer web hosting. Domains are priced at $15 per year, which is reasonable considering the exceptional level of service.

Obtaining a domain name is easy no matter where you do it, so you'll be tempted to get yours at the place that offers the cheapest price. Before you do, there's one other thing you need to be aware of: you'll have to connect the domain name to where you host your blog. If you don't properly connect the domain and the host (which techies call "mapping the domain"), it won't work, and people will have trouble finding your blog. Mapping the domain name is the tricky part, and if you're not comfortable with web technology you stand a good chance of getting frustrated or failing completely.

To avoid problems, I recommend that most of you use Hover.com to get your domain (see Figure 3.3).

Figure 3.3 Search for Domain Names on Hover

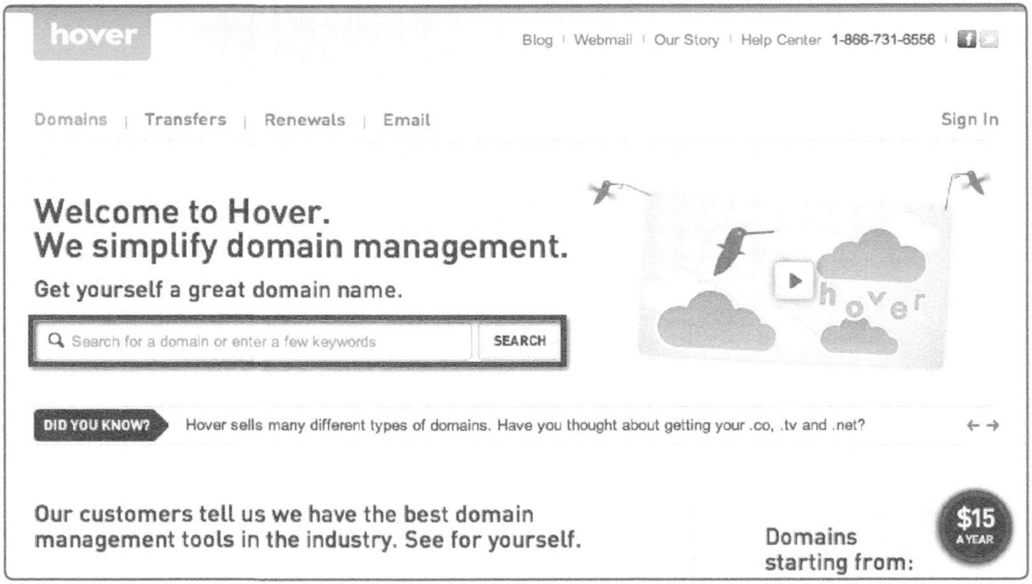

For most people, the ease of phoning and talking to a live human who will help you figure out any problems is worth the minimal extra cost. If you're tech-savvy and frugal, then by all means go with one of the other options.

Go Daddy is a popular domain registrar, so most of the blog hosts will have specific instructions on how to map your domain name from Go Daddy. However, if you have problems with Go Daddy, you'll find it will be harder to get telephone support than with Hover.

Remember: regardless of where you get your domain name, you can always transfer it to another registrar later.

Hosting: Cost and Reliability

Your blog needs a place to live on the Internet. That place hosts the software you use to run your blog, which we'll talk about in a bit. There are lots of sites that will host your blog. Some are reputable; many are not. The reputable ones tend to be a little more expensive. As a guideline, anything around $10 per month is reasonable.

What are you getting when you pay a web host? Well, a few things, but most importantly:

- **Storage for your data.** Your blog posts, and any image files you upload, are data. Data storage and management are the main things you want from a web host. Some hosts automatically back-up your data, and others do not. Automatic backup is obviously desirable.

- **Software updates.** Many hosts automatically update your blog as part of their service. While checking for updates is not difficult, it's more convenient if you don't have to remember to check.

Hosting is easy to find, but unless you're tech-savvy, not so easy to set up. Tech-savvy people sometimes offer to set up other people's sites and then throw in low-cost hosting as part of the deal. Maybe you have a friend like that, and are tempted by the offer of free (or extremely low-cost) hosting on your friend's account. Avoid this offer.

Even assuming your friend is able to provide reliable hosting, the odds are you'll regret this decision later. For example, if your friend gets busy, moves away, or gets hit by a bus, you'll face the dilemma of trying to convince the hosting company to give you access to your own blog.

No matter whom you get to help you set up your blog, make sure the host is a Tier 1 hosting company, and that the account is in your name, so you pay the bills directly. And make sure you have the login information. I repeat: make sure you keep track of the login information!

If you're planning to have a WordPress blog, you can't go wrong using one of the Tier 1 hosting companies that WordPress recommends:

- DreamHost (dreamhost.com)
- Bluehost (bluehost.com)
- Media Temple (mediatemple.net)
- Laughing Squid (laughingsquid.us)

What if you don't want to pay for hosting? Is it possible to have a blog that's absolutely free? Yes, read on.

Blogger: The Free Option

Blogger (blogger.com) is a popular blog-hosting company run by Google; it's free and provides both blogging software and hosting. You can even map a unique domain to a Blogger site. Even with those many benefits, Blogger has a stigma among many lawyers that WordPress and TypePad don't have. Blogger sites are often perceived as lacking the professional design that WordPress and TypePad sites have.

Regardless of which blog software you use, it's not a bad idea to set up an account with Blogger just to get a feel for what's possible. Blogger has a bunch of templates that you can play around with to get a sense of how you might want your blog to look. You can do all this experimenting without publishing the blog, so you don't have to worry about anyone seeing that you're working on a blog.

You have to have an account with Google to set up a Blogger website, but the accounts are free. If you have a Gmail address, then you already have an account, and Google will let you set up a Blogger account with no fuss (see Figure 3.4). If you don't have a Gmail address, you can set one up at mail.google.com.

Figure 3.4 Blogger

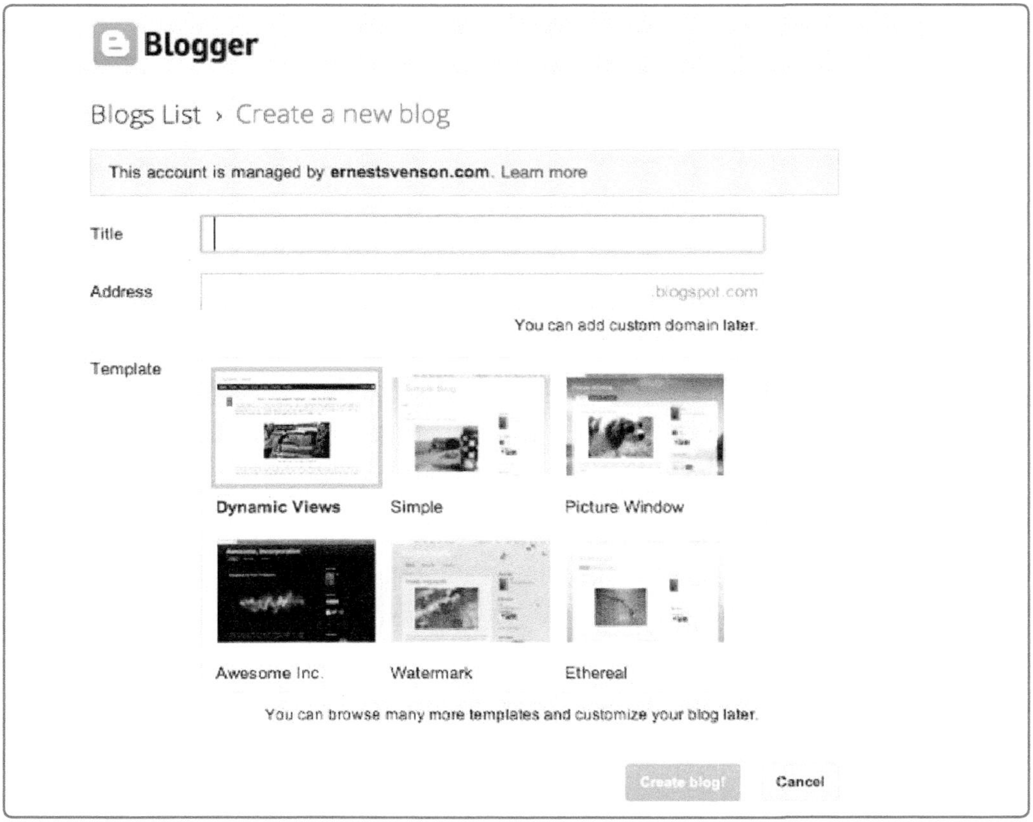

All you have to do is: (1) create a title for the blog, (2) create a unique web address (the phrase .*blogspot* will be automatically added), and then (3) pick a template. As with almost all blog software, you can change the look of the blog later without any problems. The ability to redesign a blog at any later date is possible with almost every blog software. The drawback of Blogger is that redesign is more limited, unless you really know what you're doing. So people who want the greatest design options will invariably favor WordPress.

WordPress: The Popular Option

WordPress is free, many people use it, and the hosting (provided by third-parties), isn't that expensive. If you're comfortable with web technology, or are willing to pay someone to do the setup and design of your site, you should use WordPress (see Figure 3.5).

Figure 3.5 WordPress

WordPress offers many add-ons that allow you to make your site function almost any way you want. These add-ons are called plug-ins, and they're like applications on a typical smartphone (e.g., apps that can provide such functions as creating and managing task lists, or keeping track of airline and hotel reservations). These apps change the functionality your phone had on the day that you bought it.

Plug-ins for WordPress are like smartphone apps because they allow you to extend the utility of your blog beyond its initial capabilities. When you first create a blog that uses WordPress, you might not care about adding any plug-ins. That's fine. But if a year from now you learn about some cool feature you'd like to incorporate into your blog (e.g., a banner image that keeps changing), you'll be able to add it via a plug-in. Plug-ins are a great way to make your blog work exactly the way you want it to.

If you know you're going to make a strong commitment to blogging, go with WordPress. If you don't mind paying someone to set up your blog, then I'd definitely opt for WordPress.

Regardless of the blogging tool you settle on, you want software that provides the following options:

- Easy setup, or easy-to-find setup assistance
- Easy posting and editing
- Flexible comment management (e.g., allows disabling of comments on a per-post basis)
- Good SEO (search engine optimization) features
- Multi-author posting (e.g., "Post by John" or "Post by Ernie")
- Custom domains (e.g., domain mapping, or connecting a registered domain to a web host as described in Registering Your Domain Name earlier in this chapter)

WordPress provides all these options, and many others. WordPress also allows you to import a blog from certain other platforms such as Blogger or TypePad.

TypePad: The Easiest Option

TypePad also provides all the options listed above, and because it provides both software and hosting, it's a better choice for the lawyer who is not comfortable with technology or for whom the prospect of setting up a non-hosted blog seems too challenging.

TypePad blogs are easy to set up and post to, and they are rich with features that serve the needs of professional bloggers. The company has been around for a long time and has a strong position in the world of blogging; it's reliable, and likely to remain so.

TypePad offers several different pricing options. The basic plan is $8.95 per month, which includes the software for creating posts and pretty much any features a law blogger would need. You get hosting for one blog, to which you can map a domain name that you've chosen from Hover.com or GoDaddy.com. The software for creating posts is also part of that price. You can easily create a professional look with one of the basic design templates and then modify it slightly. Complex web designs are not feasible with TypePad, but if you're not interested in extensive modification, you'll be fine with this plan.

The next level is $14.95 per month, and it allows more design customization, which assumes you know how to tweak a web design or are willing to pay someone to do it for you. It also provides unlimited data storage, which is good if you're going to be posting lots of pictures or videos. If you're not sure, stick to the basic plan; you can always upgrade later and add features as you need them.

In addition to basic hosting services, TypePad also offers professional assistance for bloggers who want to do more with their blogs, but don't want to spend the time configuring all the possible blog settings. Among the services that TypePad offers are:

- **Power Launch Service** ($349). With this service, you get help setting up and designing your blog, including help with mapping a custom domain and setting up the Google Analytics tool to measure web traffic more precisely.
- **Custom Design** (price depends on requests). This option provides help creating a custom design for your blog, including a custom banner.

These services are worthwhile in my opinion. The time it takes to map a domain, set up a blog, and tweak the design can easily amount to several hours. If you factor in the cost of your time, you may find paying Type-Pad's folks for setup and design is a cost-effective option. When I started my various blogs on TypePad, these services weren't available. Even though I know how to set up a TypePad blog, if I were starting today, I'd pay TypePad to do it for me.

Setting Up Your Blog

Let's walk through the process of setting up a TypePad blog. We'll cover how to map your domain name to the site, so make sure you have a domain name reserved (go back to Lesson 3 if you want a refresher on getting a domain name).

For those who have decided on a WordPress blog, instead of TypePad, the following pages will still be useful for understanding the typical options for a blog, and why you'd choose some things and not others.

TypePad Set Up

The first step is to use your web browser to navigate to <u>Typepad.com</u>, where you will see a page that looks like Figure 4.1.

The default instructions offered by TypePad pretty much walk you through the process step by step, so you can probably just follow those instructions. Still, it might be helpful to walk through the steps here as well.

Here's the process I used when I set up a blog related to this book.

Figure 4.1 TypePad Home Screen

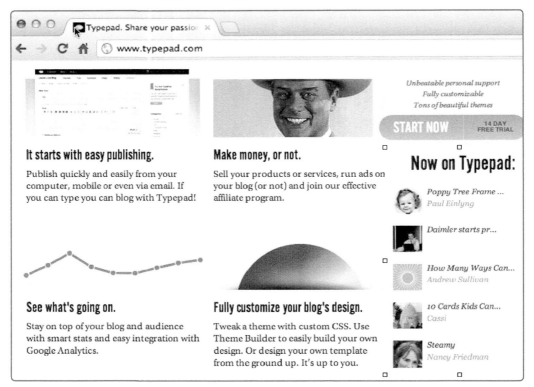

Create an Account

First, create a TypePad account with a unique login name and password. Once you're registered with TypePad, you'll be prompted to create a blog, and to give it a name (see Figure 4.2).

Type in the name you want for your blog. This is the name that TypePad will give it for now, so it doesn't need to be the same as your domain name. But, to make things easier to keep track of, I suggest you use the domain name that you've obtained from <u>Hover.com</u> or whichever domain provider you chose. For this book-related blog, I obtained the domain name <u>OneHrBlog.com</u>.

Figure 4.2 Create a Blog

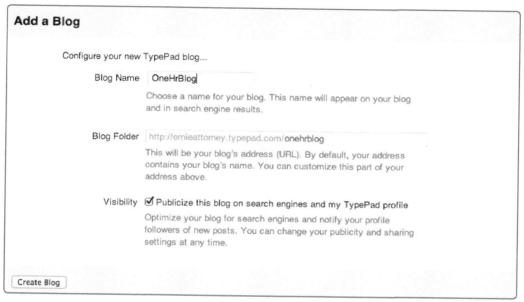

Leave the box checked next to the word **Visibility**, because you are no doubt going to want to have your blog fully publicized. TypePad will do most of this work for you if you leave this box checked. You can always go back and change this setting later if you need to.

Main Dashboard

Once you've set up your blog, you should be taken to the Settings panel, which is where you'll configure the look and basic functionality. The **Settings** panel is one of several that you can access from the **Overview** dashboard. You'll find the Settings tab on the far right of the main page for your blog (see Figure 4.3).

Click on the **Settings** tab and you'll be able to configure a series of important options.

Figure 4.3 Main Overview

Basics Panel

There are a number of key settings to tackle, so let's walk through them, one by one. After you've clicked the **Settings** tab shown in Figure 4.4, you'll notice that the various types of settings are listed in tabs along the left-hand side.

The first tab is called **Basics**, and it should already have your blog name filled in. You'll need to add a short description, which is what will be displayed in search results. Make the description succinct; people do not spend a lot of time deciding whether to click on a link to a blog, so here's your chance to influence that quick decision.

Figure 4.4 Settings Options

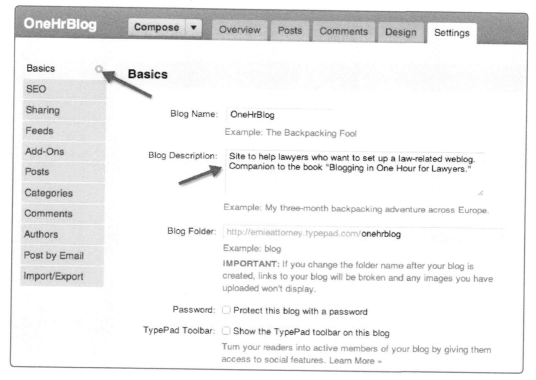

You don't want readers to have to enter a password to navigate your blog (that will ensure that almost no one reads it), so leave the **Password** box unchecked. Leave the **TypePad Toolbar** option unchecked as well; it's not helpful because it mostly helps promote TypePad. Click **Save Changes** and you're done with this section.

SEO (Search Engine Optimization)

Now click on the **SEO** tab on the left (see Figure 4.4). *SEO* stands for "search engine optimization," which is important because it tells you to how easily findable your blog is. Search engines are useful because they help people find relevant content, and they rank the content according to its authoritativeness. Google is the most popular and well-known search engine, but there are others, such as Bing and Yahoo. All search engines work pretty much the same way, analyzing the content of a particular post, the overall content on the site, and incoming links from other sites.

Before you even create any posts, you can help the search engines figure out what your site is about by providing a short description and some keywords. This is what you'll be doing in the SEO area of the blog settings.

The **Publicity** box should be checked off already, but if it's not, be sure to check it as shown in Figure 4.5. Also, you want to create a **Google Sitemap**, so check that option, too.

Figure 4.5 SEO Options—Part 1

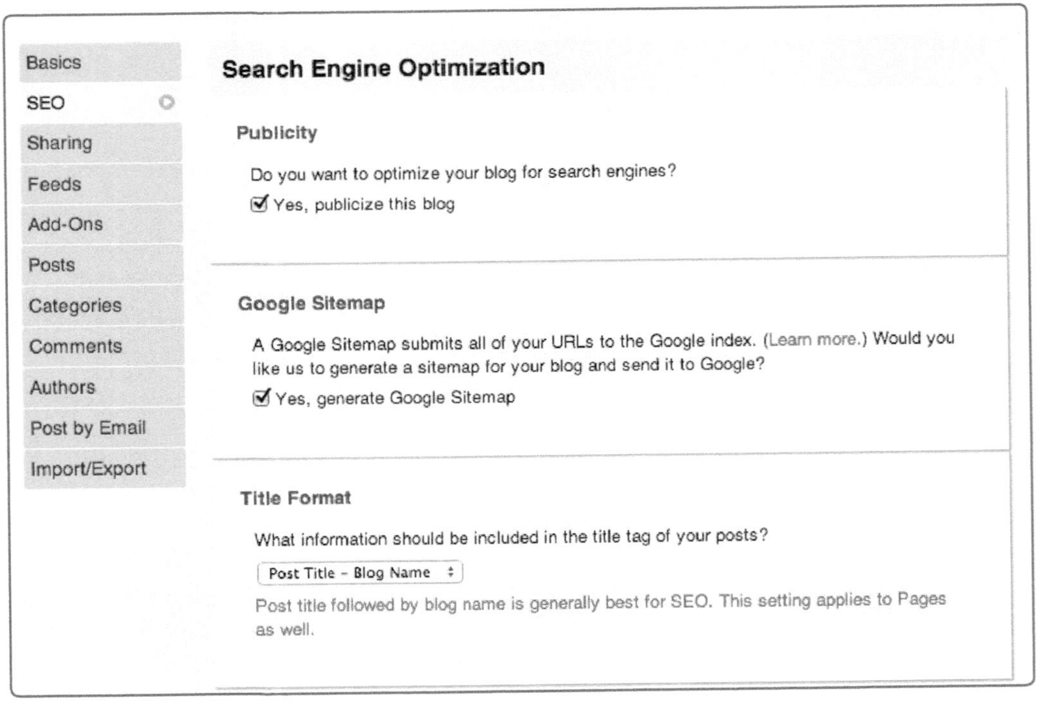

Basics	**Search Engine Optimization**
SEO	
Sharing	**Publicity**
Feeds	Do you want to optimize your blog for search engines?
Add-Ons	☑ Yes, publicize this blog
Posts	
Categories	**Google Sitemap**
Comments	A Google Sitemap submits all of your URLs to the Google index. (Learn more.) Would you like us to generate a sitemap for your blog and send it to Google?
Authors	☑ Yes, generate Google Sitemap
Post by Email	
Import/Export	**Title Format**
	What information should be included in the title tag of your posts?
	[Post Title – Blog Name ⬍]
	Post title followed by blog name is generally best for SEO. This setting applies to Pages as well.

Leave the option for **Title Format** as it appears, pre-selected to "Post Title—Blog Name." As I mentioned, TypePad tends to steer you toward the important options that most bloggers want to have by presetting some of the options for you.

Let's keep working down the SEO page options. Next is some key information that will encourage people to click through to your blog. Take your time coming up with the text for these input fields (see Figure 4.6).

Figure 4.6 SEO Options—Part 2

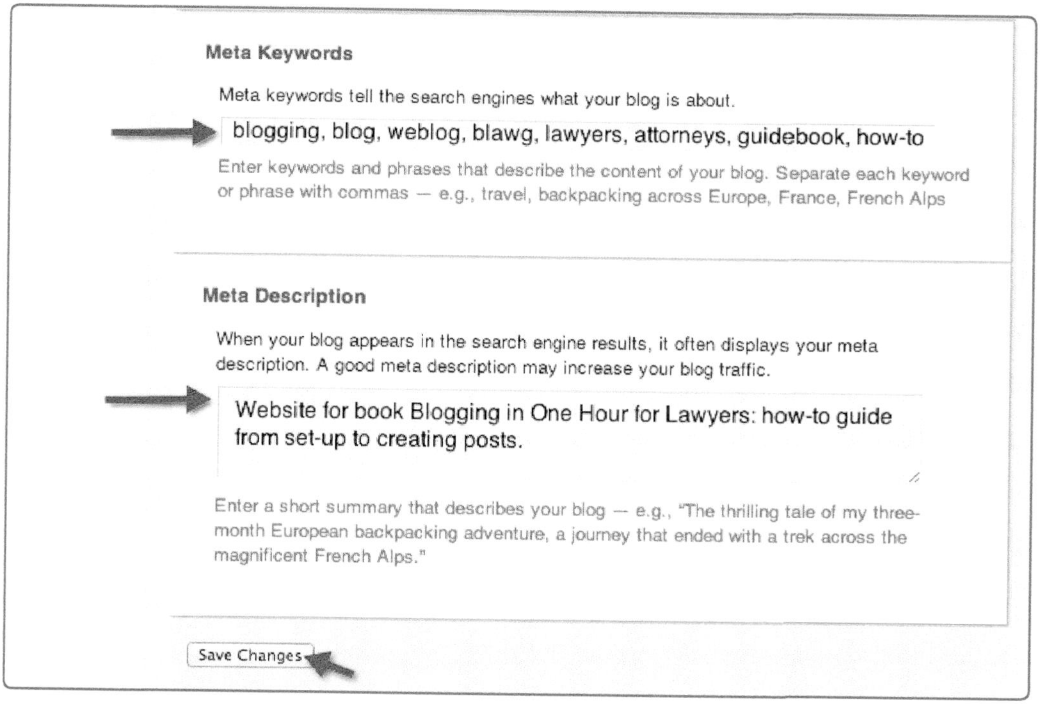

The **Meta Keywords** field allows you to enter words or phrases that define what your blog is about. Figure 4.6 shows how I described the website for this book.

For the **Meta Description** input field, create a very short blurb. Google uses the first 20 to 25 words of this description in search results, but if it's more than 25 words, Google may create its own snippet. You can always change it later, so for now see if you can describe your blog in 25 words or less. You see from Figure 4.6 that my description took only 18 words.

Once you've made all the entries, click the **Save Changes** button.

Sharing

Click the **Sharing** tab (see Figure 4.5); you should see a screen like the one in Figure 4.7.

Figure 4.7 Sharing Options

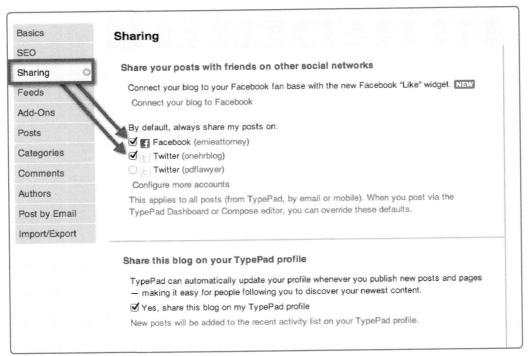

If you have a **Facebook** page, you can connect it to your blog so that anytime you post to your blog, your Facebook page is automatically updated with the post. Sometimes the paragraph breaks get removed when it winds up on Facebook, so the result often isn't pretty. Don't worry if you don't have a Facebook page. This isn't a critical connection to make, at least not in the beginning.

The **Twitter** connection, on the other hand, is important. If you have a Twitter account, then making a connection allows TypePad to automatically generate a tweet whenever you publish a new blog post. Even if you have a Twitter account already, you should set up a new one because you want to tie your blog to a related Twitter account, not your personal one.

Ideally, you should get a Twitter account with the same name as your blog's domain name. Figure 4.7 shows that I have checked the box for the Twitter feed I created for this book. You'll note that the Twitter name (a.k.a. the "Twitter handle") for my account is exactly the same as my blog's domain name: onehrblog. You'll also notice that I didn't connect to my PDF for Lawyers Twitter account, because that's not related to the blog for this book.

Why should you use Twitter to help publicize your blog? Simple. Because Twitter is the best way for people to keep up with small news tidbits. More than 200 million people are on Twitter, and it's an easy audience to write for (you're limited to 140 characters). Twitter accounts are free to set up; all you need is a verified e-mail address. If you want more information on how to use Twitter, read the book *Twitter in One Hour for Lawyers*, by Jared Correia.

Once you've configured the accounts you want to connect to, click **Save** and you're done.

Feeds

The **Feeds** tab is where you decide which part of your web content you want to syndicate as an RSS feed (see Figure 4.8). The acronym *RSS* stands for "really simple syndication." RSS is an important tool, and its power cannot be overstated. Many web surfers have learned to harness RSS so that it automatically pulls new content from blogs and websites, mostly by using an RSS reader. One of the most popular readers is the free Google Reader.

Figure 4.8 Feeds Options

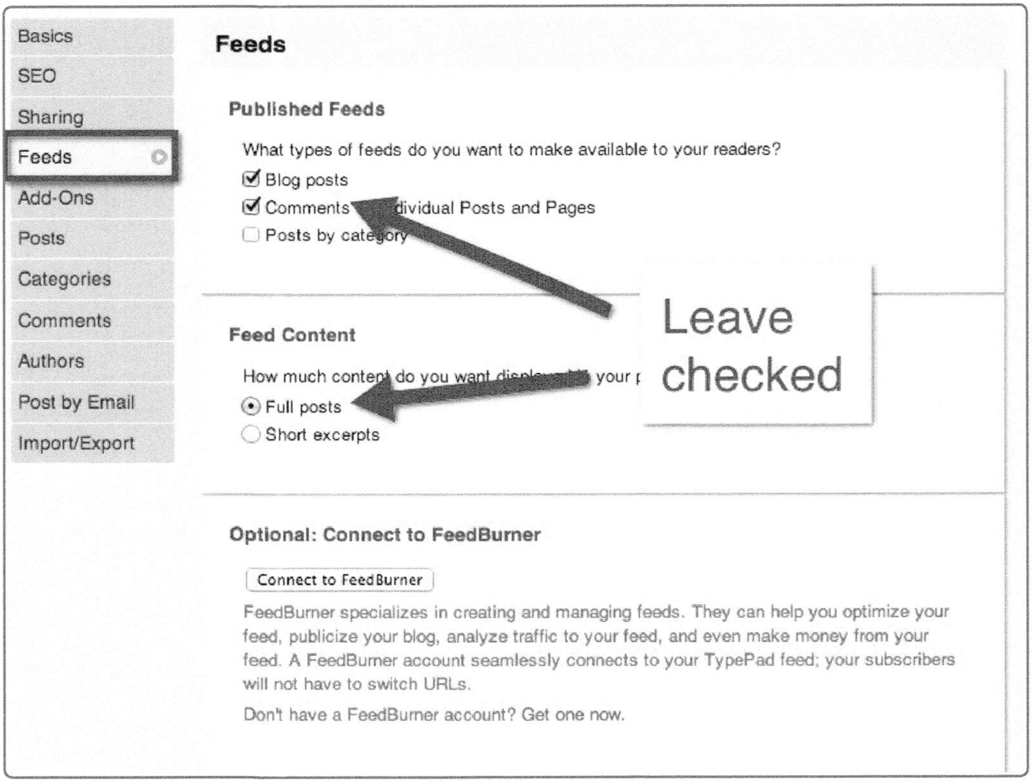

Many people who will follow your blog will do so in an RSS reader, which enables them to automatically pull new content from your blog without having to open their browser, navigate to your main page, and then scan new content. For people who want to read content from several blogs, the RSS reader is indispensable. So, under the heading Published Feeds, leave the **Blog posts** option checked.

Do you want to allow readers to post comments to your blog? And do you want to allow readers to subscribe to those comments? If so, leave the box next to **Comments on Individual Posts and Pages** checked.

Next, you have to decide how much of your content you want to syndicate. Some people believe it's better to entice people to visit their site, so they only post short excerpts of their blog posts. Doing so annoys people who use RSS readers since it defeats a key benefit—not having to take the time to open a browser and navigate to your blog. While commercial websites seeking a high traffic count to get an advertising advantage have a plausible reason for delivering excerpts, lawyers who want to build a strong audience should deliver an RSS feed comprising the full post. So, under the **Feed Content** heading, click the **Full posts** option. Then click **Save Changes**.

To summarize: we've just accepted the default options in this section. Skip the Add-Ons tab and let's move now to Posts.

Posts

This section lists lots of choices, but only the first two require discussion. I recommend you accept all the default choices as shown in Figure 4.9.

Figure 4.9 Posts Options

The **Default Publishing Status** should generally be set to Publish Now because you're probably going to want to post immediately after you've created the post. The **Draft** option is for posts that you're working on and planning to edit. If you want to have your publishing status always set to Draft, check that box instead.

In the next section you'll decide how many posts will appear on your home page. Remember that a key feature of a blog is rolling content: old posts roll off the home page as new ones are added. So, you have to determine when the old content gets archived.

The default setting is for 10 posts, but you can bump that number up or down. You can also configure your settings so that only posts within a certain number of days—the last 30 days, for example—are displayed.

But it usually makes sense to set the cut-off based on the number of posts. That way, if you don't post regularly, you always have something on your home page. Leave the display to the default of **10 posts** for now; you can always change it later.

Ignore all the other choices and just click **Save Changes** to accept the defaults.

Categories

When you create a post you're given the option to classify the post into a given category. You can create new categories as you post, but **Categories** is where you set up the categories you're most likely to use often (see Figure 4.10).

Figure 4.10 Category Options

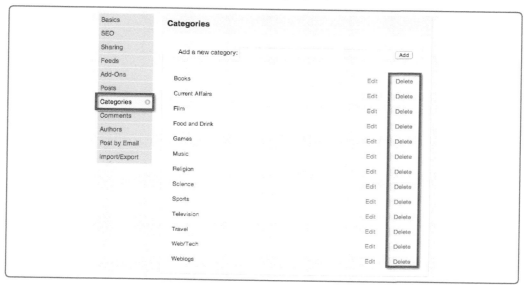

The default categories in TypePad are pretty generic. My suggestion is to delete them all and create new ones. For example, you might have categories such as: "court decisions, legislation, legal commentary," or whatever topics correspond to the theme of your blog.

Be careful about having too many categories. You want to have just enough categories so that every post fits into at least one of the categories; some posts will fit into more than one. What you don't want is to have a few categories that have only one or two posts after you've been blogging for years and have hundreds of posts. Each time you post, you need to remember to assign categories for the post; it's not done automatically.

For more information about categories, read this Knowledge Base article on TypePad's site: http://help.typepad.com/blog_settings_categories.html.

Comments

Comments are useful for most blogs because they promote discussion among your readers. The downside of comments is that there are some readers who are more interested in provocation than rational discussion. That's why some bloggers don't allow comments.

Most, however, allow comments that they moderate themselves. You have the option to approve comments and to require commenters to disclose something about who they are. For example, you can require them to sign in using TypePad, Facebook, or Twitter, but this can get annoying and discourage people from leaving comments. So, leave the **Optional** button checked. In short, most of the default settings in this section are the ones you want (see Figure 4.11).

Figure 4.11 Comment Options—Part 1

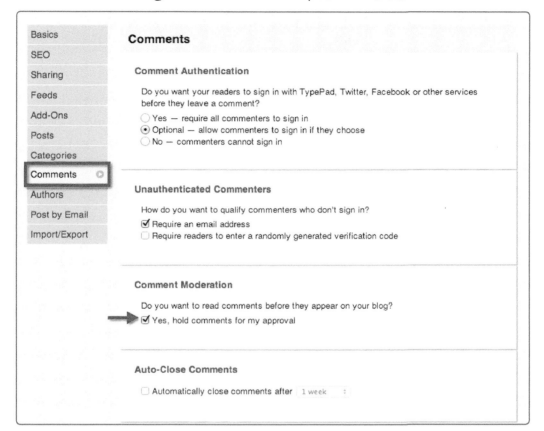

For **Comment Moderation** you should select the option **Yes, hold comments for my approval** so no one posts anything inappropriate without your knowledge. You should not disapprove comments simply because you disagree with the point of view. But, you should review the comments before they go up for everyone to see.

Leave all of the rest of the default choices in place, but let's cover a couple of choices that you'll find at the bottom of this section that you should at least have a passing acquaintance with (see Figure 4.12).

Figure 4.12 Comment Options—Part 2

Email Notification
☑ Notify the author of the post when new comments are submitted
☑ Notify the author of the post when new TrackBacks are submitted

By default, accept comments...
☑ On new posts
☐ On new pages

By default, accept TrackBacks...
☐ On new posts
☐ On new pages

If you use comments, then you probably want to be notified when people post comments. So, leave the option selected (see Figure 4.12) that says "Notify the author of the post when new comments are submitted." And if you want comments, choose **By default, accept comments**.

What about TrackBacks? A TrackBack is a link that someone puts on your site in the comments that points back to theirs. The idea was that, if I read your blog post on a topic I had written about, I could point people back to my post. At first, TrackBacks were quite popular. Then, to paraphrase Yogi Berra, they got so popular that no one uses them anymore. In other words, they got popular with spammers. If you allow TrackBacks, you're just allowing your site to be exploited by spammers in ways that will degrade it.

So **DO NOT** check either of the two boxes related to TrackBacks, as shown in Figure 4.12.

Authors

The last tab we will cover is **Authors**, which is only necessary if your blog will have more than one person (author) posting to it. TypePad assumes that the person who owns the blog is the main author, and gives that person complete rights. But blog owners can authorize other people, if they choose (see Figure 4.13).

Figure 4.13 Author Options

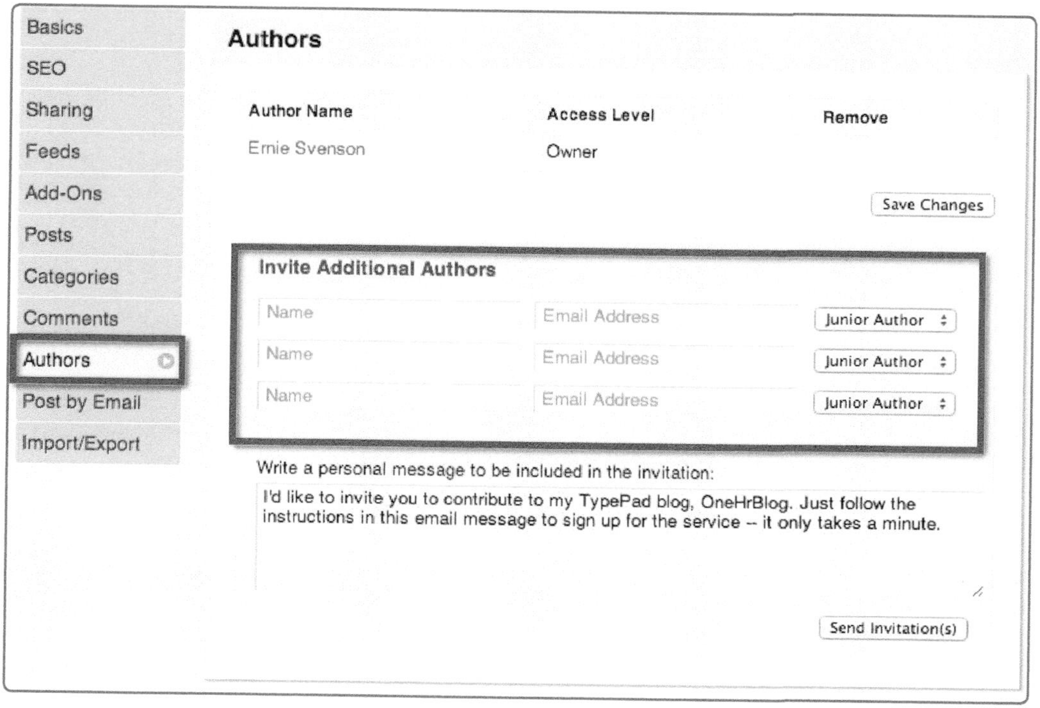

The default setting for new authors is **Junior Author**, which does not allow them to post without your approval. If you want your co-authors to have the right to post on their own you can select **Guest Author**. Having a blog that several people can post to can be very beneficial, so you aren't the only one responsible for updating. As the owner of the blog you can revoke rights at anytime, or change the level of rights granted.

Domain Mapping

Next we'll map your domain name to your blog, so people can find it using that domain name. I obtained the domain <u>onehrblog.com</u> for this book, so I'll demonstrate how to map a domain in TypePad using that example.

In TypePad we start the process by going up to the top right of the <u>TypePad.com</u> webpage (after logging in). There you should (1) select the **Account** tab, and then (2) select **Domain Mapping** from the left-hand menu, as in Figure 4.14.

Figure 4.14 Select Account Tab and Domain Mapping

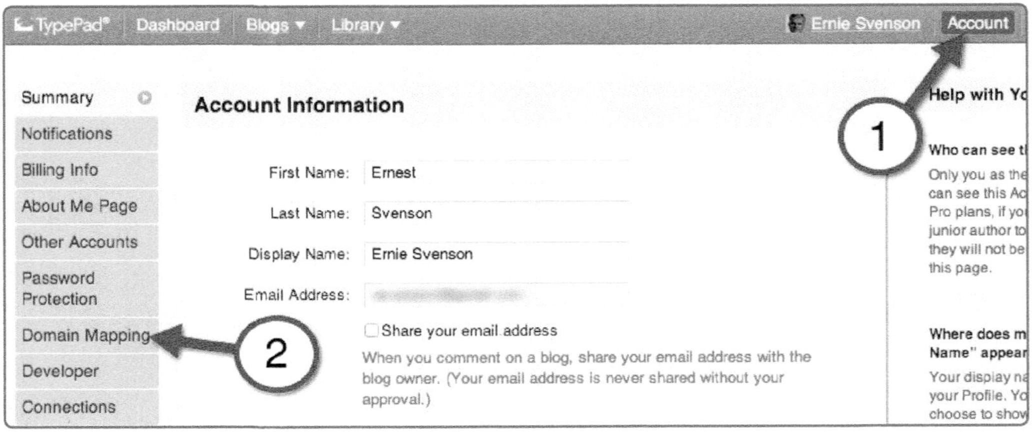

You'll then be presented with stern warnings like the ones in Figure 4.15.

Figure 4.15 Domain Mapping Warning

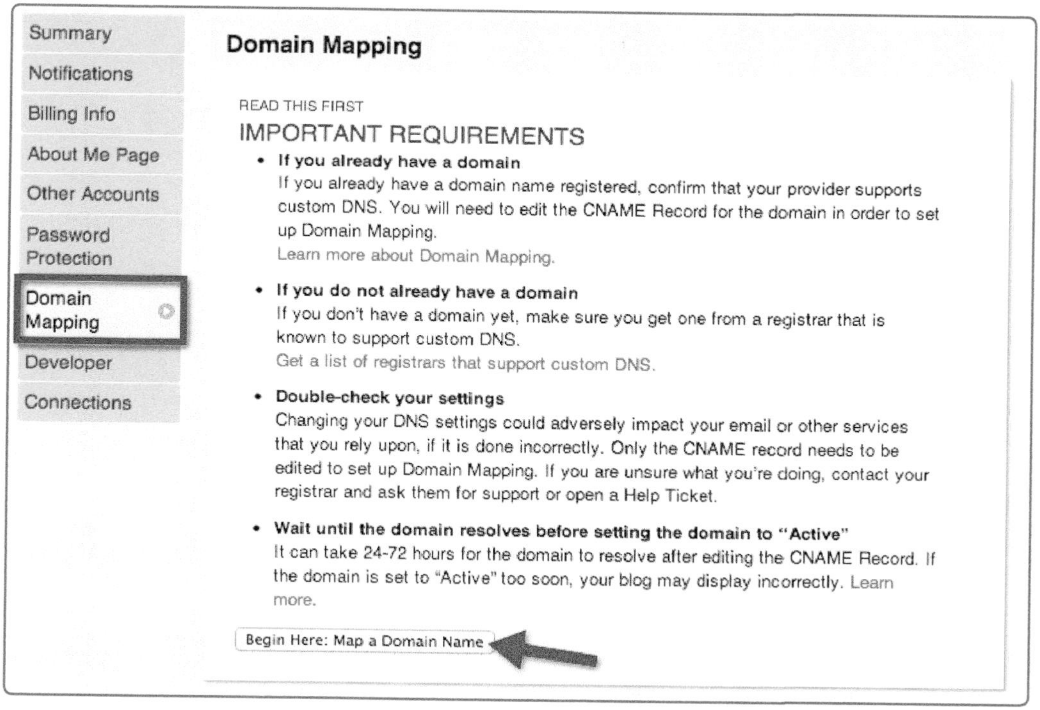

Obviously, you need to have already acquired a domain, and if you got it from <u>Hover.com</u> or <u>GoDaddy.com</u>, then you should be able to edit the CNAME record easily. So, click the button that says **Begin Here: Map a Domain Name**. You will see what appears in Figure 4.16.

Figure 4.16 Add Domain Mapping

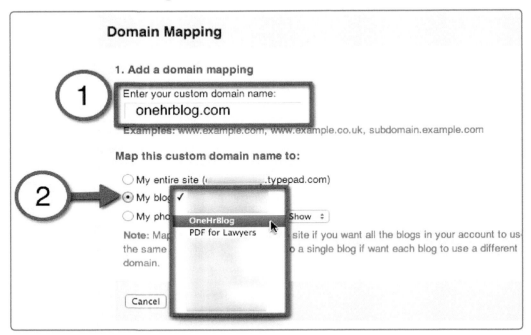

Enter the name of your domain (you don't need to enter *www*), and then move to the next option. You can have your entire site mapped to the new domain. Because I have several blogs hosted at TypePad, I was asked to choose which one I wanted to map. I chose the OneHrBlog, as opposed to the PDF for Lawyers blog (which is already mapped). After you make these changes, you'll be taken to the next screen (see Figure 4.17).

At this point, you'll have to navigate over to the provider from whom you acquired your domain. In my case, that's <u>Hover.com</u>. But regardless of your provider, you're looking for the CNAME record at your domain registrar. It will be under a tab named **DNS Settings**. If you use Hover and you can't easily find this tab, you can call the support line and someone will walk you through the process. (In case you're wondering, a CNAME record is an alias for a domain name that points it to another host name.)

Figure 4.17 Get CNAME Record

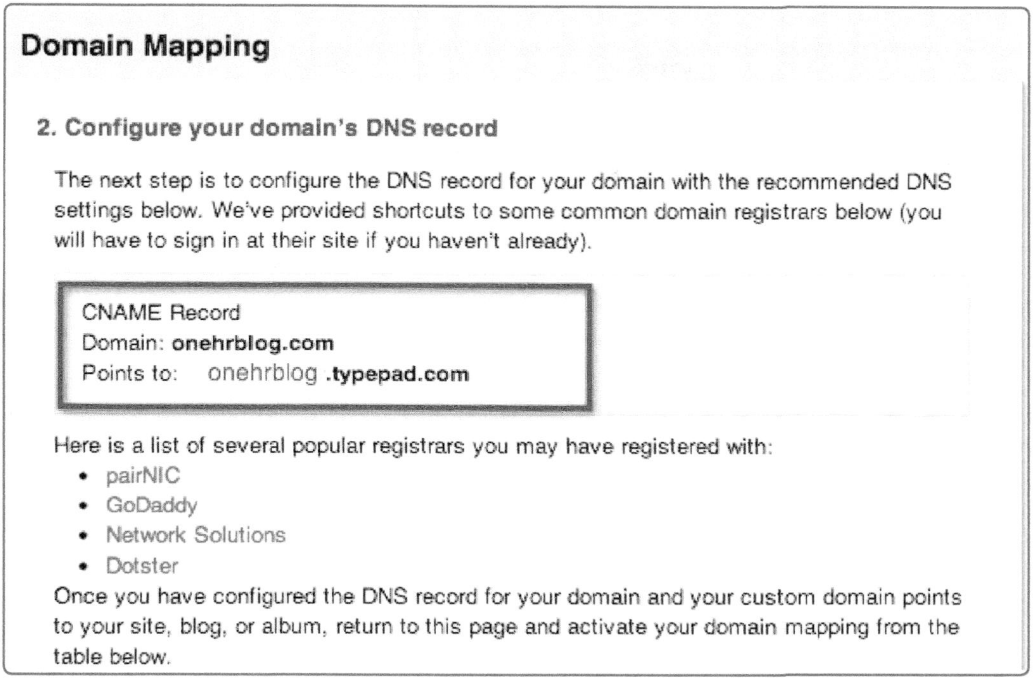

Domain Mapping

2. Configure your domain's DNS record

The next step is to configure the DNS record for your domain with the recommended DNS settings below. We've provided shortcuts to some common domain registrars below (you will have to sign in at their site if you haven't already).

> CNAME Record
> Domain: **onehrblog.com**
> Points to: onehrblog **.typepad.com**

Here is a list of several popular registrars you may have registered with:
- pairNIC
- GoDaddy
- Network Solutions
- Dotster

Once you have configured the DNS record for your domain and your custom domain points to your site, blog, or album, return to this page and activate your domain mapping from the table below.

You'll point it to whatever name TypePad has listed next to "Points to:" In Figure 4.17, the name is *onehrblog*, which is my blog domain name. Whatever verbiage you see, select and copy it so you can paste it into your domain registrar's CNAME record. (It's important to get this verbiage matched up exactly, so if you write it down make sure you copy it correctly.) The CNAME settings will be in an area that relates to DNS, which is short for "domain name servers."

Click on the **DNS** tab (see Figure 4.18) to open up **Settings**, where you can add or change the CNAME record. Figure 4.19 shows a CNAME record for "mail." This is for e-mail, if you want to have an e-mail address for the domain. You need to add one for a website, which is designated by the familiar *www.*

Figure 4.18 Edit DNS Record—Part 1

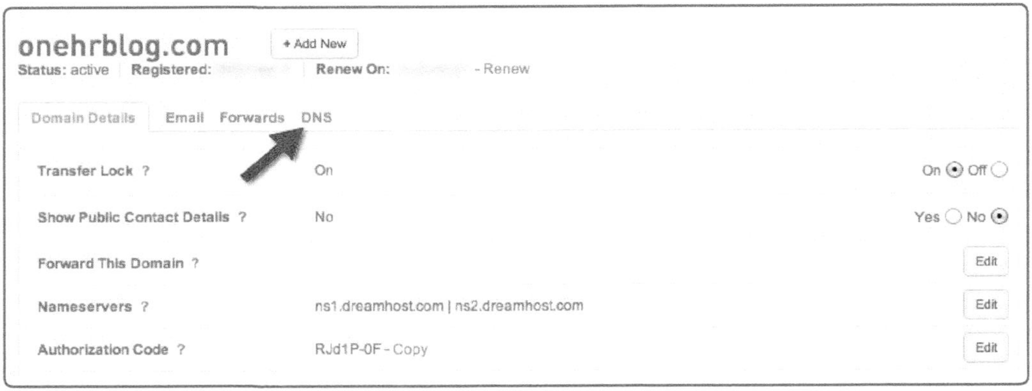

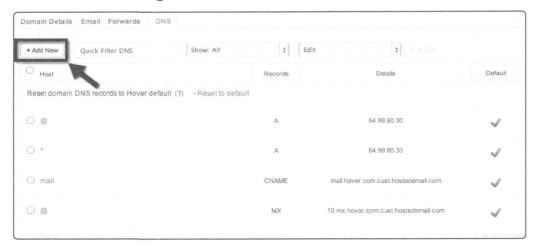

Figure 4.19 Edit DNS Record—Part 2

Once you click the **Add New** button, or whatever the method is for a domain provider other than Hover.com, you'll see a screen like Figure 4.20.

Figure 4.20 Edit CNAME Record

onehrblog.com
Status: active | **Registered:** 2012-06-07 | **Renew On:** 2013-06-07 - Renew

Domain Details   Email   Forwards   DNS

Hostname ?	Record Type ?	Target Host ?
www	CNAME ↕	defaultname.typepad.com

For **Hostname** enter "www" (without the period). Under **Record Type**, set the selection to CNAME. Finally, under **Target Host**, enter the name that TypePad gave you as the address to "point to." It will be the default name followed by "typepad.com."

Save the change and go to the main page. One other thing that Hover requires is to forward the domain, which you do in the **Domain Details** tab, as depicted in Figure 4.21.

Figure 4.21 Domain Forwarding

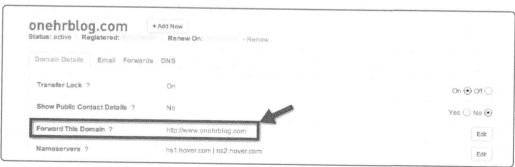

onehrblog.com   + Add New
Status: active | Registered: Renew On: - Renew

Domain Details   Email   Forwards   DNS

Transfer Lock ?	On	On ⦿ Off ○
Show Public Contact Details ?	No	Yes ○ No ⦿
Forward This Domain ?	http://www.onehrblog.com	Edit
Nameservers ?	ns1.hover.com	ns2.hover.com	Edit

Enter the full URL of your domain name (i.e., include *http://*) in this area. Save those changes and then wait for the domain redirect to propagate through the Internet. Sometimes the changes happen within a few hours, but usually it takes between 24 and 48 hours. So, just be patient.

Figure 4.22 shows what my blog looked like once the redirect kicked in.

Figure 4.22 Verify Domain Mapping

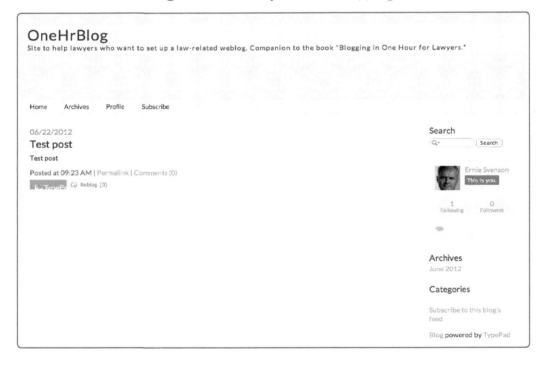

Once you see the skeletal TypePad blog page (Figure 4.22), you're ready to go back to the **Account > Domain Mapping** area and confirm to TypePad that the domain name redirect is active. You'll see a screen like Figure 4.23, and under the **Actions** column you just have to click the word **Activate**.

Figure 4.23 Activate Domain Mapping

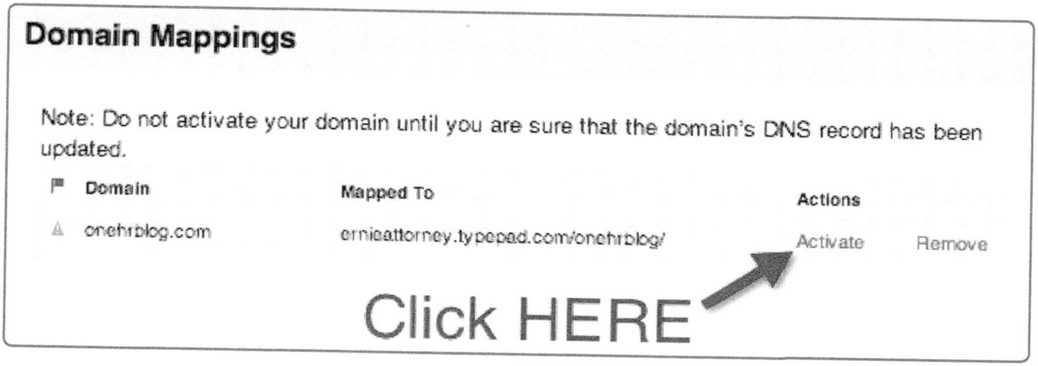

Domain Mappings

Note: Do not activate your domain until you are sure that the domain's DNS record has been updated.

⚐ Domain	Mapped To	Actions	
⚠ onehrblog.com	ernieattorney.typepad.com/onehrblog/	Activate	Remove

Click HERE

If you have any problems with the domain redirect, go back and make sure you have followed the directions from TypePad correctly. If you have, the next step is to call <u>Hover.com</u> because, as I said, their phone support is truly phenomenal. Even if the problem is in the TypePad setup, the folks at Hover won't brush you off; they'll try to help you figure it out. But you may have to e-mail TypePad support if the Hover support people can't troubleshoot the problem.

Once you can reach your blog by typing in the domain name, you can assume that other people can see it too. At this point it's time to dress up your blog so it looks a little more interesting.

Designing Your Blog

You want your blog to be visually appealing, to both you and your readers. The best design is clean and simple, one that makes it easy for people to find what they're looking for. Since the default templates will almost always be clean and simple, using one of them is a good option; then you can fiddle with the basic design a bit to distinguish your blog from the thousands of others that use the same software.

We'll discuss how to make basic design changes on TypePad and WordPress, but if you can afford design help for your blog, I recommend you get it. TypePad offers comprehensive design consulting services on a per-quote basis (quotes are free).

Help designing a WordPress blog can be found on a site called oDesk.com, which is akin to eBay for web-related services. You bid out the job you need help with, and people around the world compete for it. Although it's the cheapest way to get web services, it does require that you be comfortable working with someone you've never met and providing precise directions to someone who may not be a native English speaker.

For now, though, we'll cover the basic adjustments you can make easily on your TypePad blog.

Banner and Colors

On TypePad, start by clicking on the **Design** tab, which will open the design panel (see Figure 5.1).

Figure 5.1 Design Tab

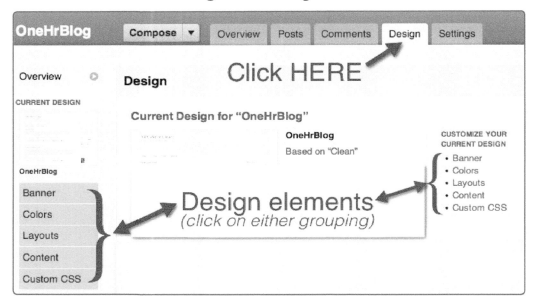

First, decide if you want to customize your banner by putting an image behind your text. I have one that includes a background image of the proposed cover design for this book. If you aren't familiar with image editing tools like Adobe's Photoshop Elements, leave the blog banner as it is. The next step is to choose your colors. I'll pick the **Clean – White** option, but you can choose one of the other five options (see Figure 5.2).

Figure 5.2 Color Choices

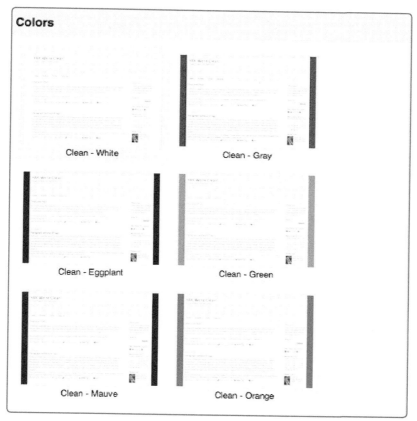

Layout

The **Layout** option determines how many sidebars you have. Although some blogs have multiple sidebars, most have only one, and that's probably the best option for you. It can appear on either side of the page; I'll leave mine on the default setting, which is the right-hand side (see Figure 5.3).

Figure 5.3 Layouts

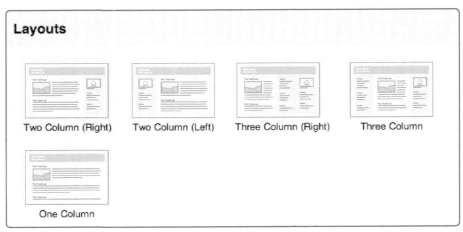

Content

Next, you'll choose the elements that you want to appear on your blog, whether in the main section or in the sidebar(s). Figure 5.4 shows the four sidebar elements that I recommend you eliminate.

Figure 5.4 Sidebar Content

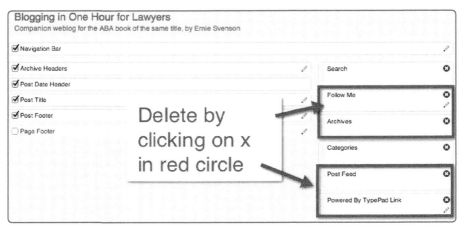

You don't want the **Follow Me**, **Archives**, or **Post Feed** options because those are duplicates of links in the navigation bar. And you don't want the **Powered By TypePad Link** because that's duplicated at the bottom of the blog.

Next, let's change the **Navigation Bar** slightly. Click on the **pencil** icon at the right, as shown in Figure 5.5.

Figure 5.5 Navigation Bar Content

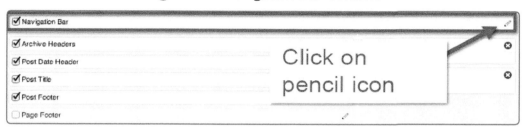

You'll then see a screen like Figure 5.6.

Figure 5.6 Navigation Bar Edit Window

Navigation Bar Configuration

⦿ Simple   ○ Advanced

Enter up to ten links to display in your navigation bar.

	Title	URL
1	Home	⊦ .... typepad.com/onehrblog
2	Archives	.... .typepad.com/onehrblog
3	Profile	http://profile.typepad.com/⦁ ....
4	Subscribe	http://ernieattorney.typepad.com/onehrblog

You can change the name of a **Title** by deleting the default content and entering your own. For example, for number 3, you can change the Title from "Profile" to "About Me." You could change the hyperlink as well, navigating, for example, to your LinkedIn profile page.

LinkedIn is the optimal tool for creating a public profile. Your LinkedIn profile is much more than just an online resume, and I encourage you to set up an account if you haven't done so already. I also recommend you take a look at Dennis Kennedy and Allison Shield's excellent book, *LinkedIn in One Hour for Lawyers*, to learn how to get the most out of LinkedIn.

If you have a Twitter account to go with your blog—and I recommend that you do—you can add a navigation link that goes to your Twitter page. In Figure 5.7, you see the result of the editing I did to my Navigation bar.

Figure 5.7 Edited Navigation Bar on Website

Remember to hit the **Save Changes** button anytime you make changes, or they won't show up on the webpage, and you'll have return to the editing window to make them again. Failing to save changes is a common mistake, which you can expect to make more than once. The good news is that, once you've made all the changes we've covered, you're done designing your blog. Now, it's time to post content.

Posting to Your Blog

Once you've got your blog set up, it's time to start putting up content. I'm going to continue to demonstrate this process using TypePad, but WordPress, or any other blog software, offers the same options. This lesson will help you understand the mechanics of posting to your blog, no matter what software you use.

Your First Post

Before you begin entering text into the composition window, make sure that your **editing** option is set to **Rich Text**, as opposed to HTML. Rich Text is the WYSIWYG option (which means, "what you see is what you get"), and it allows you to see what the content is going to look like on the web as you're writing. TypePad, Blogger, and WordPress all have WYSIWYG options.

Once the editing option is selected, it's time to create your first post, which can be something trivial since you're only testing whether content is properly uploading to the web. Figure 6.1 shows what a typical test post would look like in TypePad. You'll want to create a title and some body text.

Figure 6.1 First Post (Test)

As Figure 6.1 illustrates, you begin by clicking on the **Compose** button and then proceed to add a title and some text in the body. Next, make sure you've selected Published, and not Draft (otherwise your test won't be visible on the web), and then click on the **Publish** button (see Figure 6.2).

Figure 6.2 Submit for Publication

Once you've submitted the post for publication, your web browser should take a few seconds and then automatically refresh. You'll still be in the editing window, however, so you'll have to click **View blog** in the top right as shown in Figure 6.3.

Figure 6.3 Click "View blog"

At this point your browser should open up in a new window (or new tab, if that's how your browser is set) and you'll see the results on the web (see Figure 6.4).

Figure 6.4 Web View of Post

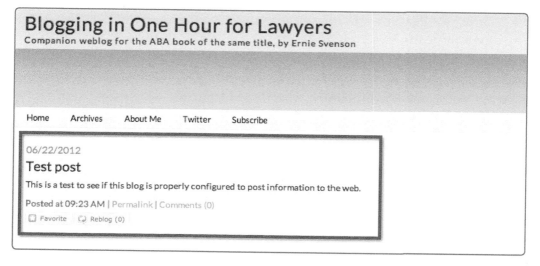

Do you see your content on the web? Congratulations! You now know how to post content to your blog so that people can read it. Now let's discuss some of the basic options you have to format your posts.

Basic Formatting

The editing window of your TypePad blog has a toolbar like the one in Figure 6.5. Let's focus first on the most basic formatting options.

Figure 6.5 Basic Formatting

The first choices are those most common to all blog software and familiar word-processing tools. You can use these buttons (in the red box in Figure 6.5) to bold, italicize, or underline text. You can also set the justification of the text to left margin, centered, right margin, or full justification. You apply formatting just as you would with any word processor: you select the text you want to format and then click the appropriate formatting button. You can also format headings (as you would with Styles in a word processor like Microsoft Word), as well as the font, and font size (see Figure 6.6).

Figure 6.6 Font Style Formatting

Use the **Indent** button (at the left side of the box in Figure 6.7) to indent a paragraph, and select the button next to it to remove indenting. You can also create subscript or superscripts (right side of the box in Figure 6.7).

Figure 6.7 Indent

If you want to change the color of a font or create a highlight, you have those options as well (see Figure 6.8). There is an option to create a strikethrough, which is text that has a line through it. Some people use strikethrough to signal that they were thinking of using, say, a ~~silly~~ certain phrase, but then changed their mind (as I just did). You can also remove all formatting if you want by clicking on the eraser icon to the left of the strikeout button. These options are boxed in red in Figure 6.8.

Figure 6.8 Font Color

If you need to create an indented block quote, or create bullet points, you can do that as well (see Figure 6.9). The points can be either numbered or bulleted.

Figure 6.9 Block Quotes and Bullets

Although odds are you won't use most of these tools regularly, they provide a lot of control over how your text appears. The important thing to remember is that they're there. And if you forget what a given button does, just hover your mouse over it and pause until a pop-up description of the tool appears.

Let's move on to some of the more sophisticated tools that take you beyond formatting.

Uploading Multimedia Files

No doubt you've seen websites that include pictures within an article, or that allow you to download files. You can add those features too. All blogging software allows you to upload images, video, audio, and any kind of file that you want your readers to be able to download. Figure 6.10 shows the buttons you use in TypePad.

Figure 6.10 Multimedia

I would caution against uploading video to your blog because the file sizes tend to be large and the bandwidth required for readers to view the video is large as well. Audio files can be useful, but they can also be large; for the most part you should upload only short clips of audio or video.

Uploading files, however, is a useful option in many cases. For example, if you have a PDF document you want people to be able to access, you can upload it and include a link that people can click to download or view the document. The process for uploading files is almost identical to the process for inserting images, which I will illustrate next.

Inserting images may not be something you'll do often, but this feature is important for any blogger to understand. The **Image** button is on the far left in the red box in Figure 6.10. When you click on it, you'll be asked to select and then upload an image. At that point, you can either accept the default options, or alter the size of the image and choose where you want it to go (see Figure 6.11).

Figure 6.11 Image Upload

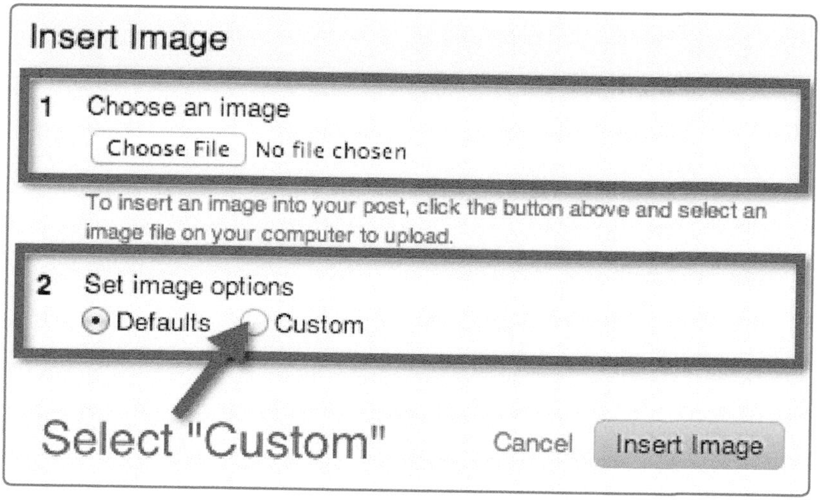

I recommend you choose the **Custom** option so that you can resize the image and place it where you want it. Once you've selected Custom, you'll see the dialogue box shown in Figure 6.12.

Figure 6.12 Custom Image Options

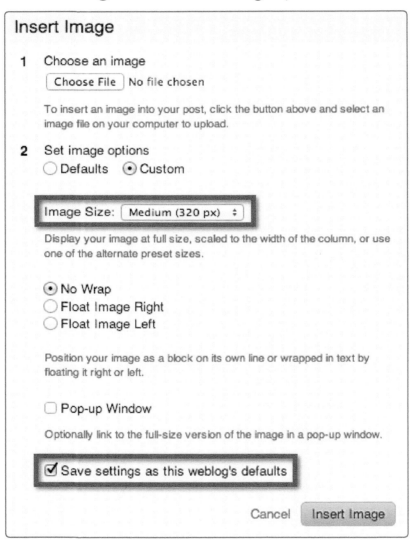

For TypePad users, I recommend using the medium image size (320 pixels) as the default setting. After you select the **Medium** option, check the box at the bottom to **Save settings as this weblog's defaults**. Then, click the **Insert Image** button to upload the image into your post, which will also save the settings as a default. From now on, you'll only need to choose the **Custom** option if you want to change the size of the picture or where it's placed.

Figure 6.12 shows the image option set to **No Wrap**. If you want the text to wrap around your picture, then choose one of the other options, depending on which side you want the text to wrap around. Often, you'll simply put a picture in the middle of your post and not wrap the text. To get the picture to appear in the middle, place the cursor on one side of the picture and click the **Center Justify** button on the toolbar (see Figure 6.5).

Hyperlinks

The most important button for bloggers, including lawyers who blog, is the button for creating hyperlinks. All of the other buttons are about making your blog look attractive, and providing useful or memorable content. In TypePad, as in all blogging software, the icon for the hyperlink will be a image of a chain link (see Figure 6.13).

Figure 6.13 Hyperlinks

The **Hyperlink** button is your secret weapon for getting attention. If your blog isn't getting enough attention, you probably aren't using this button enough. In this section, I'll demonstrate how to create a hyperlink, and show you how to strategically utilize it.

Figure 6.14 is a sample post that offers lawyers some great blogs to read. Note that I've directed them to Jim Calloway's excellent blog (which, by the way, is a TypePad blog). The post mentions the blog, but I haven't provided a link.

Figure 6.14 Post without Hyperlink

Novice bloggers tend to put links into a post as shown in Figure 6.15.

Figure 6.15 Post with Awkward Hyperlink

The better option is to select the text "Jim Calloway's Law Practice Tips Blog" and then click the **Hyperlink** button so that those words become a hyperlink. Figure 6.16 shows the dialogue box that pops up when you do that.

Figure 6.16 Creating a Proper Hyperlink

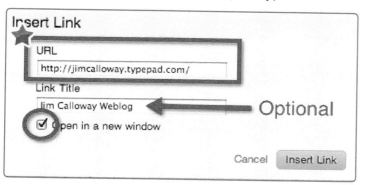

To create the hyperlink, you have to copy the URL from the browser address bar and paste it into the URL field of the dialogue box. You can create a **Link Title** as well, but it's not necessary, and many bloggers (I'm one) don't do this because it only appears if you hover over the link, which most readers don't do. Click the box **Open in a new window** if you want the hyperlinked page appear in a new window (and you almost certainly do) when readers click on the link. The reason you want hyperlinks to open in a new window is to encourage readers to stay on your site as long as possible.

Once you've clicked the **Insert Link** button, you'll see the hyperlinked text change color, which signals it's a live hyperlink (see Figure 6.17).

Figure 6.17 Proper Hyperlinked Text

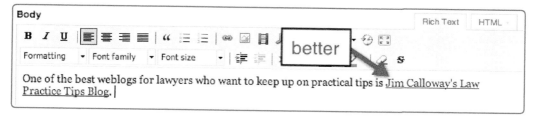

Now that you know the method for creating a hyperlink, let's talk about the strategy of hyperlinking. One strategic use of hyperlinks is to link to other bloggers. The more you link to them, the better the odds that they'll link back to you, increasing your blog traffic (which will tend to boost your site's ranking in search results). But other blogs aren't the only sites you should link to—you'll want to link to lots of different types of information on the web. Sometimes you'll be linking to a source that supports a point you're making. You might also link to a source that provides more detailed information on a subject you've referenced so you don't have to take the time to write a more complete explanation.

The key point is that it's important to start thinking about hyperlinks as you draft your posts. The more experienced bloggers have honed their linking skills, and you'll want to do the same. From now on, pay careful attention to the many ways other bloggers use hyperlinks.

Spell Check

The final step before you post anything is to go over the post closely and make sure you don't have any spelling errors. The **Spell Check** button is perhaps the second most important button after the hyperlink button. Figure 6.18 shows how it looks in TypePad (in other blog software it looks identical).

Figure 6.18 Spell Check

Unfortunately, spell check can't be run automatically. You should cultivate the habit of always running spell check before you publish any post or save a post as a draft. We'll cover saving drafts next.

Save Draft

Many times you'll start a post and not have time to finish it. Or maybe you need time to think about additional points you want to make. Either way, the post is not ready to be published. For a TypePad blog, saving a post as a draft simply requires a slight modification of what you did when you created a test post (see Figure 6.2). Go to the **Status** menu and select **Draft** (see Figure 6.19). Then click **Save**.

Figure 6.19 Save as Draft

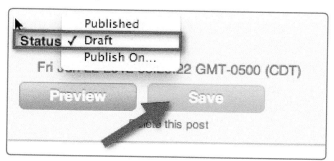

In addition to saving posts as drafts, you can also set posts to be published at a particular time and date in the future (see Figures 6.20 and 6.21). WordPress has this functionality as well, and the method for delayed posting is similar to the one used by TypePad.

Delayed Posting

To specify a future time and date when a post will be published in TypePad, go to the **Status** menu and select **Publish On** (the third option) (see Figure 6.20).

Figure 6.20 Publish Later

When you select this option, you'll automatically be presented with a pop-up window like Figure 6.21.

Figure 6.21 Set Time and Date

In Figure 6.21, the date has been changed to 8/28/2013, at 9:00 a.m. (which was in the future at the time this screenshot was taken). Creating posts to publish in the future is a great way of scheduling content that's not time-sensitive, queuing up a stream of content that will automatically go off as needed.

For example, if you're going to give a speech, it might make sense to write up a blog post that goes live the week before the speech. If you create the post as soon as you're contacted to do the talk, you won't have to worry about creating the post later when you might be too busy.

Categories

We talked about Categories in Lesson 4, which covered how to set up your blog. If you want to assign your post to one or more categories, you can do so in the post window (see Figure 6.22).

Figure 6.22 Categories

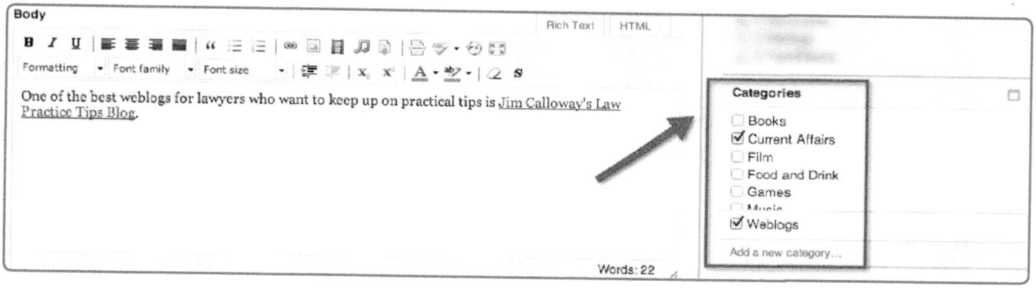

I've selected two categories to associate with this post; if I wanted to I could add more. As I mentioned in Lesson 4, categories should be few in number so you don't wind up with categories that have only one or two posts associated with them. Some supposed SEO gurus would tell you to pick categories that are likely to show up in searches for your blog's overall topic. My recommendation is that you limit your initial choice of categories to topics for which you're certain to have multiple posts. You can add categories later to deal with new subtopics.

Notify Twitter and Facebook

When you post new content to your blog, you want as many people as possible to learn about it and to forward it to other people they know. I recommended earlier that you set up a Twitter account with a similar name as your domain name. All blog software allows you to easily share your post via Twitter and Facebook, and TypePad is no exception.

If your **Share This Post** setting is configured to share content with Twitter and Facebook, you'll see a section that looks like Figure 6.23 just below the area devoted to Categories.

Figure 6.23 Notification to Twitter and Facebook

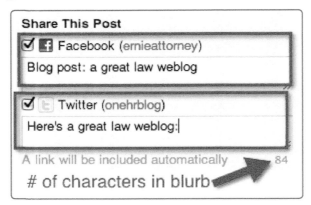

Check the box next to Facebook if you want to post there and then create a short blurb that will appear on your Facebook page. If you don't have a Facebook page, don't worry about it. It's more important to use Twitter as a notification tool. Facebook can only notify your friends, while Twitter notifications can reach anyone who uses Twitter.

To post to Twitter, check the Twitter box and enter a short blurb describing your post in a way that will entice people to check it out. TypePad will let you know how many characters you have entered as you type. Twitter only lets you use 140 characters, so keep the blurb as short as you can. A link to your blog post will be inserted behind your blurb. Keep in mind that the characters in that link will also count toward your 140-character limit. TypePad uses the <u>Bit.ly</u> link shortening service so your links will only consist of 13 characters, meaning you have 127 at your disposal.

Keywords and Technorati Tags

Adding **Keywords** to your posts can help search engines better categorize them. If you don't include Keywords for an individual post, the Master Keywords you entered for **Settings > SEO** in Lesson 4 will be used for the post. Keywords will not display on your blog; they're just there for search engines. Figure 6.24 shows the Keyword entry box.

Figure 6.24 Keywords

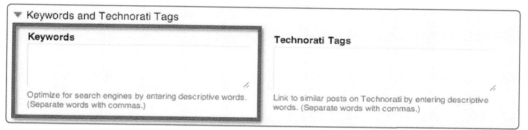

Google no longer gives much value to keywords, and it can be reasonably assumed that other search engines will follow suit. So, you may not want to take the trouble to use the Keywords option.

You can also enter **Technorati Tags** in the box to the right, as shown in Figure 6.24. Technorati is an Internet search engine specifically focused on blogs, and it has indexed more than 100 million blogs. TypePad automatically registers your blog with Technorati, but it doesn't automatically add Technorati tags. That's up to you to do, but it's generally not that helpful in improving your search rankings.

Comments

Many bloggers don't allow comments, which obviates the problem of having to moderate them. In the initial set up, you made the determination about whether you want people to be able to post comments. But with each post you can override, or modify, that choice. Figure 6.25 shows the options you have with each post.

Figure 6.25 Comments and TrackBacks

Because I have set comments so they are automatically allowed, the **Open** box is checked by default. If I don't want to allow comments, I choose **Closed**. Also, if I had allowed comments for a time, but now want to cut them off I can choose Closed, and only past comments will be allowed and visible. If you don't want comments to be visible at all, check **Hidden**.

Whether you allow comments or not may be determined by the kind of blog you plan to have. For most blogs that provide general commentary it makes sense to at least experiment with comments. In the early stages of your blog you have a lot of latitude (because you have fewer readers), so that's the best time to find out if comments are helpful. Comments are a great tool for creating stronger reader engagement, but if your readers tend to become too provocative, you may be better off without comments.

There's no real choice about TrackBacks. As I mentioned in Lesson 4, you never want to allow TrackBacks. Having TrackBacks does nothing useful for your site, and will certainly attract spammers. So, always leave the TrackBacks option set to **Hidden**.

Pages

You can create pages on your blog that are different than posts, because they're static. Pages are like traditional web pages on a website, and can be used to publish content that you want to remain in place. For example, you could use a page to create an "About Me" description or to publish a disclaimer. The process of creating pages is the same as for creating blog posts. Once you've created a page, you have to get the link and then publish that link wherever you'd like (usually that would be in the navigation bar, as explained in Lesson 5).

To create a new page in TypePad, click the **Compose** button (see Figure 6.1) and select **New Page**. You don't want to have too many pages because it's cumbersome to administer the links to pages you create.

Multiple Authors

Most blog software allows you to have multiple authors posting to a blog, each with their own login credentials. If you want to give authors credit for their posts, you can have the software do that automatically.

TypePad authors can have different levels of permission for posting. To configure additional authors in TypePad, go to **Settings > Authors** (see Figure 4.13).

Updating Posts

Sometimes you need to update a post because you found some typos or small mistakes. Other times you'll need an update because you've received new information you want the post to include. The question in each case is whether you can just edit the post and not signal to anyone that you've changed it.

For small changes (e.g., typos and small mistakes) go ahead and make the change without notification. If the typo is something that changes the entire meaning of a sentence, you may want to edit it by striking through the ~~old~~ misleading word (as I just did).

When you have new information, simply editing the post could be misleading, as someone may have quoted the old post elsewhere on the web; if someone else were to read that account and then navigate to your blog (i.e., the source), the person who linked to you would look foolish because the source would be different from the quote.

To avoid this situation, you can add an entry at the bottom of your post labeled "Update" and provide an explanation of the new information you want to share.

Sometimes novice bloggers think that they can make changes without repercussion if the changes are made quickly after the post was first published. That would be a reasonable conclusion if there were no RSS feeds. Once you publish a post, it is sent to RSS readers that are subscribed to your blog and are running. Your change may not get sent to the RSS reader, or any number of things may conspire to make your mistake a permanent fixture on the Internet, even though you corrected it immediately.

In short, it's best to assume that anything you've published will be out there somewhere in its original form forever. So, make sure you edit carefully, run spell check, and even delay posting to give yourself as many chances as possible to catch and correct errors.

Getting Attention and Monitoring It

Now that you've created your blog, you want to drive traffic to it. But getting traffic isn't enough; you also need to know how much traffic you get and where it comes from.

Write Well

The best way to get attention is to write great posts about interesting topics. Most important, avoid jargon; don't use the writing style you use for legal briefs. Write crisp, readable sentences and you'll draw in casual readers and convert them to loyal ones.

Craft punchy headlines that entice readers to read the first sentence of the article. Then write a compelling first sentence; make it short. Edit ruthlessly. Remove all unnecessary words.

Someone once observed that the perfect blog post is a two-paragraph observation. While there are no hard-and-fast rules in blogging, a two-paragraph post is probably the sweet spot, and a good guideline for a new blogger. The first paragraph should tantalize the reader and set up the main point; the second can expand it slightly, making strategic use of hyperlinks.

The importance of hyperlinks cannot be overstated. They're the life-blood of all online writing, helpful for linking to sources, explanations, or definitions. Short block quotes of key passages from a text, followed by a hyperlink, are frequently used by successful bloggers, who know that people who surf the web are easily distracted. You must cultivate that awareness too, employing resources that make your points quickly.

The more often you post, the quicker you'll get the hang of it. Study other bloggers, and keep working on improving your technique. There are no shortcuts to learning how to write compelling blog posts.

Register Your Blog

Once you've published a handful of posts, you're ready to let the world know about your site. And by *world* I mean search engines, which will be the way most people discover your blog. If you set up a TypePad blog, then you took care of this when you checked the box that said, "yes, publicize this blog." (See **Settings > SEO** in Lesson 4.)

If you're on a WordPress blog, or if you just want to be sure all the key search engines know about your blog, register with these sites:

- Google: https://www.google.com/webmasters/tools/submit-url
- Bing: http://www.bing.com/docs/submit.aspx
- IceRocket: http://www.icerocket.com
- Blogarama: http://www.blogarama.com
- Ping-O-Matic: http://www.pingomatic.com

You should also register with such law blog directories as the following:

- ABAJournal.com/blawgs: the most prestigious list of U.S. law blogs
- Canadian Law Blogs: http://www.lawblogs.ca/submit/

- <u>Justia.com</u>: 6,755 blawgs in 75 subcategories
- <u>Blawg.com</u>: 4,333 active blogs
- <u>USLaw.com</u>: asks for a voluntary post of one of their graphic linkbacks
- <u>Lexmonitor.com/blogs</u>: a large list of law blogs, but registration may be limited
- <u>BlawgRepublic.com</u>: a real-time search engine that monitors the legal blogging community every hour
- <u>BlawgReview.blogspot.com</u>: features one blog every month

E-mail Newsletter

The easiest way for people to get your new blog posts automatically is an e-mail newsletter, especially helpful for web-surfers who don't know how to use RSS readers. Many new bloggers have a knee-jerk reluctance to setting up an e-mail newsletter, convinced they lack the time to put one out every week.

A service like <u>Feedblitz.com</u> will pull your RSS feed and generate an e-mail newsletter automatically. All you have to do is connect Feedblitz to your RSS feed and set up a delivery schedule. Usually, you'll want to set the newsletter to go out no more than once a week, maybe even once a month in the beginning.

The price of Feedblitz varies depending on how many people you have subscribed to your blog, but it is reasonable and well worth the investment. Remember, when people subscribe to your e-mail they're giving you their e-mail address, something extremely valuable from a marketer's perspective. If you don't fully appreciate this (and I certainly didn't when I started out), read Seth Godin's excellent book, *Permission Marketing: Turning Strangers Into Friends And Friends Into Customers.* It will teach you the basic theory of why e-mail marketing is so powerful.

I can't emphasize this enough: if you're serious about blogging, set up an e-mail newsletter.

RSS Feed

As noted previously, many people will follow your blog using an RSS reader, automatically pulling new content from your blog as it's published. You'll want to know how many people are following you in an RSS reader, and basic blog tools like TypePad or WordPress won't give you that number. To get this information, you can sign up for a Feedburner account (run by Google), which will provide you detailed statistics about how many people are reading your blog using an RSS reader, what sort of RSS reader they're using, and where in the world your RSS readers are located.

Monitoring Site Traffic

Keeping tabs on the traffic your blog attracts is essential to using your blog strategically. Knowing how many hits per day your blog gets is a crude measure. You want to know more, such as:

- **How many page views you get.** This is the number of web pages that people visit on your site. To encourage people to visit more pages you should link, wherever reasonable, to previous posts.
- **Page views per visitor.** This tells you how "sticky" your site is. These are people who look at more of your content than just what they find on the home page, or wherever they first landed.
- **Unique visitors per day.** If you get 100 visitors to your site, but one person visited the site 20 different times you want to filter that out. (It was probably you checking the look of your blog!) You want to know how many different people came to your site in a given time period.

TypePad has built-in tools that monitor your blog's traffic, and you can see an example of the screen for my PDF for Lawyers blog in Figure 7.1.

Figure 7.1 Blog Statistics

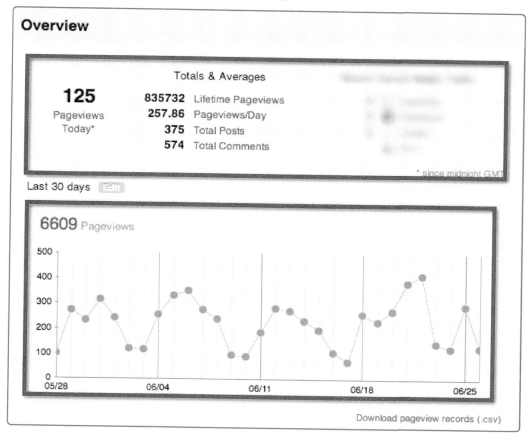

The raw numbers in the top section show **Lifetime Pageviews**, **Total Posts**, and **Total Comments**. The big number at the left (125) is the current day's Pageviews. The lower section is a graph of **Pageviews** over the last 30 days.

Sites that link to your blog are called Referrers, and TypePad, like all other blog tools, tracks those referrers. On the **Overview** page for your blog you get limited statistics about what sites are linking to your site, or otherwise delivering readers. When you notice a site delivering significant traffic, add it to your list of RSS feeds (see Lesson 8). Any site that is sending you a lot of hits is one you should pay close attention to, since that site's owners are obviously paying close attention to you.

In addition to sites that link to your blog, you can also monitor search strings that led to your site, discovering what search terms lead people to your site. Consider posting more content with those terms, since they seem to have a higher web profile and will draw more traffic to your site.

What's a proper amount of web traffic? It depends on your blog. Your focus should be on increasing your readership among those who are most passionate about the topics you cover. For some topics that might be a hundred people, and for other topics it might be several thousand.

If you want more detailed statistics about your web traffic, you can use tools like SiteMeter (sitemeter.com) and StatCounter (statcounter.com). These services operate through software code placed on your site, which generates detailed reports regarding behavior of your blog's visitors, such as the first and last page each visitor looked at. Both tools offer free and premium services.

Google Analytics

Since no one has a cyber-finger on the pulse of web traffic more firmly than Google, most bloggers use Google's analytic tool to obtain more detailed web traffic information.

Google Analytics (at google.com/analytics/) is free for basic information—how people found your site, how they explored it once they got there, what time they arrived, and how long they stayed. The more sophisticated analytics tools, including Google's, will show you what browser your readers used to access your site.

If you have set up a TypePad blog, you'll want to check out the Knowledge Base article on configuring your blog to include Google Analytics: http://help.typepad.com/google_analytics.html. To configure your TypePad blog to work with Google Analytics, go to the **Settings** tab and select **Add-Ons** (see Figure 7.2).

Figure 7.2 Google Analytics

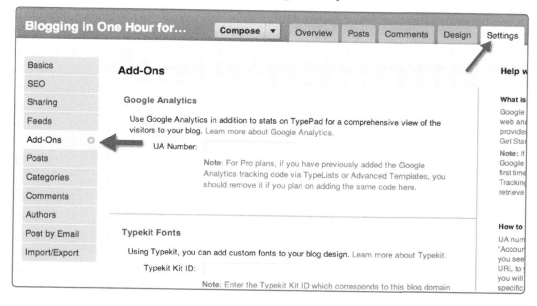

Or you can sign up for the Power Launch service ($349) and the people who work at TypePad will help you set up the Google Analytics as part of that fee.

Google Alerts

Google Alerts is a free service that allows you to specify a search you want Google to run, notifying you periodically with results. You can take advantage of this tool to learn via e-mail alerts what others are saying about you and your blog.

To set it up, go to google.com/alerts and enter the search you want to run. Specify how often you want be notified (once a day, once a week, or as it happens) and provide an e-mail address for receiving the alerts. As always, save the options you selected.

You may want to consider setting up several alerts. Here are some to consider:

- Mentions of your name (Practice searching until you find a string of words that yields results that relate to you—and not just someone with your same name—and use that string when entering your search.)
- Mentions of your corporate clients' names (limit the scope to news reports)
- Mentions of your blog
- Mentions of the most critical topics your blog covers

Writing for Search Engines

Writing content that humans find interesting is the most important thing you can do to raise your blog's profile. Simple adjustments will also make those posts attractive to search engines.

Remember that many of your first-time visitors will find your blog while searching the web, not while looking for your site in particular. That's why it's important to draft posts that make you as findable as possible via search engines.

Here are three effective strategies:

- **Craft each post around one central theme.** Identify a keyword that captures that theme, and use that keyword in the post as naturally as you can. If the keyword is forced, it will look awkward and put off readers. If you can't make it look natural, don't do it.

- **Use the keyword(s) in your title.** Here again, use caution. It's more important to create interesting titles that generate curiosity and heighten the attention of your would-be readers. If you can weave in the keywords, then do it.

- **Be creative with the words you use to link to other sites.** Search engines don't just look at where the link points, but also what the link says.

Twitter—Use Often

We've covered how to use the TypePad feature that lets you quickly post to Twitter as you're getting ready to launch a blog post. But if you set up a Twitter account, you should post to Twitter much more often than you post to your blog. Ideally, your Twitter feed should put out at least three posts per day, more in the beginning when you're trying to get your blog noticed.

Coming up with a regular stream of interesting and well-written blog posts can be time-consuming, but it's important; a steady stream of content will continue to engage people who've begun to pay attention to your blog. That's why Twitter is so valuable.

If you haven't been using Twitter, now is the time to start. Make sure to get a Twitter account dedicated to your blog, and use it only for posts that relate to the themes of your site.

Obviously, you'll use Twitter to announce when you've created a blog post (TypePad will do that automatically if you set it up, and so will WordPress).

There are a couple of time-saving tricks for finding and distributing Twitter content, and you should avail yourself of them right off the bat:

- Use a program like **TweetDeck** (tweetdeck.com, now owned by Twitter) that lets you monitor many different channels of Twitter content, and then easily re-tweet it (i.e., forward a tweet) into your stream. It's free software that runs on your computer, and works on both Macs and PCs.
- Use a service called **Buffer** (bufferapp.com), which allows you to dump time-released tweets and links you want to push into your Twitter stream on a schedule that you set up. The basic service lets you buffer 10 tweets for free. It also lets you schedule posts to Facebook and LinkedIn.
- **SproutSocial** (SproutSocial.com) is a step up from Buffer, and the entry level price is $9.99 per month. Use this tool if you can afford it, because it lets you manage up to 10 social media accounts, such as Twitter, Facebook, and LinkedIn, and it provides more robust analytics.
- Learn to use link-shortening services like **Bit.ly** (Bitly.com) to conserve as many of your 140 characters as possible. Buffer has link-shortening built in, as do most of the advanced social media management services.

There's a lot to learn about Twitter, most of which can be learned as you use it. One thing you should know about immediately is the notion of "retweeting." People who follow you on Twitter can easily forward any of your tweets to their followers simply by selecting the "retweet" option. Retweeting is like forwarding e-mails, but easier, so people do it more often. If you're tweeting about something that you hope to have retweeted, do not use the full 140 characters; people who retweet often like to add their own commentary, so you need to leave them room. If it's too much trouble to comment, they'll be disinclined to retweet.

Most importantly, don't use Twitter to overtly promote yourself or your practice. First, it doesn't work well and will quickly cause people to "unfollow" you, or not pay attention to you. Second, it puts you closer to ethical trouble if your state has strict rules on advertising.

Here's a tweet that a divorce lawyer sent out, which is a perfect example of how to provide helpful information without putting unnecessary focus on one's own blog:

"Divorce rate for people older than 50 doubled in the last 20 years, and baby boomers account for 1 in 4 divorces today. ow.ly/bRy4a"

By providing a steady stream of useful information about issues affecting marriage (with a proper short link to the source article), his followers grasp that he's a well-informed lawyer who practices domestic law, and—more importantly—one who can be respected.

Which lawyers should you follow on Twitter? That depends on what kind of information you're looking to harvest, but here's a short list to get you started:

- SCOTUSBLOG—@scotusblog
- Kevin O'Keefe—@kevinokeefe
- Bob Ambrogi—@bobambrogi
- Dan Pinnington—@danpinnington
- Jim Calloway—@jimcalloway
- Lee Rosen—@leerosen
- Cloudigy Law—@cloudigy
- Sharon Nelson—@sharonnelsonesq
- Wall St. Journal Law Blog—@wsjlawblog
- Tom Mighell—@tommighell
- Ed Adams—@edadams
- ABA Journal—@abajournal

Subscribe to and study those Twitter streams and you'll quickly grasp how to tweet most effectively.

ROI—How Do You Measure?

In the advertising business there's a common customer complaint: "I know half my marketing strategies work, but I don't know which half." Like any businessperson, you'd like to know the return on your investment of time. While there is no easy way to measure this precisely, anecdotes and thoughtful reflection can give you a sense of whether your blog is beneficial.

After you've been blogging for 18 months or so, ask yourself these questions:

- Is your professional reputation being enhanced?
- Is your network of professional relationships growing?
- Are you establishing yourself as a subject matter expert in areas your blog covers?
- Are some clients telling you that they're aware of your blog? If so, odds are it's helping you get and keep clients.
- Are you getting not just new clients, but high-quality clients? People who hire you because they did their own research and found information that made them feel comfortable with you tend to be easier clients to work with.

Dealing with Criticism

Once you've been blogging for a while, you can expect to get criticism. Here are the most reasonable options for dealing with criticism of your blog.

- Ignore the online statement completely. This is almost always the best option. At a minimum, set a rule that you won't comment for at least 48 hours after you first learn of the criticism.

- If the comment appears in another blog's comment section, wait the 48 hours and post a reply to the comment, explaining your position. If the initial comment was unreasonable or unjustified, aim your reply at reasonable readers, not the unreasonable person who posted the initial comment.

Remember that potential clients have access to all online information, and may use it to assess you. Rash and defensive responses to criticism will not help your marketing efforts. You want to appear confident and unmoved by pettiness.

Gathering Information

Maintaining a regular publishing schedule is key to a blog's success; the more content you push out, the more readers you'll attract. Novice bloggers recoil at the notion of publishing a lot of content, especially those already busy practicing law.

Subscribe to RSS Feeds

The secret weapon that virtually all law bloggers use is the RSS reader. By using an RSS reader you can automatically pull content from blogs that provide relevant information, which you can quickly survey and flag for follow up. There are lots of different types of RSS readers, but the best one to use is Google Reader, which is free.

If you have an account with Google, select the **More** menu and then choose **Reader** (see Figure 8.1).

You'll be taken to a Welcome banner, below which are sample feeds from popular blogs. Once you find feeds you're interested in, you can subscribe by clicking the **Subscribe** button (see Figure 8.2).

Figure 8.1 Selecting Google Reader

Figure 8.2 Subscribing in Google Reader

You can also enter a particular feed, or search for a feed that you know by name. In the example above, I input "iphonejd," which is a popular blog about use of iPhones and iPads in the practice of law. Note I didn't include ".com" after the name, because I want the RSS feed, not the website. If you enter that text string, you'll be taken to a page of results for blogs with similar names. You'll see the number of people who are subscribing to that blog and how often, on average, the blog publishes posts (see Figure 8.3).

Figure 8.3 Search Results in Reader

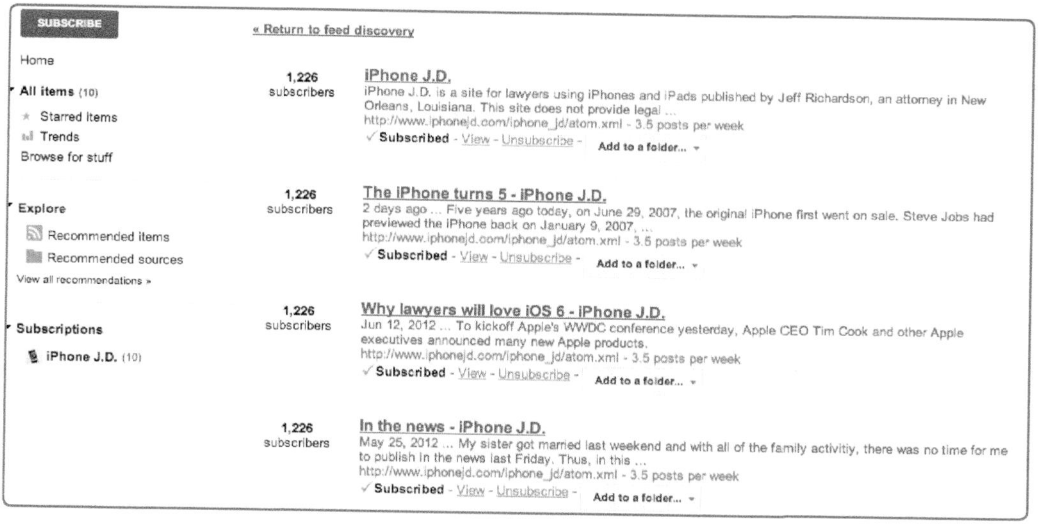

Once you subscribe to the feeds you want, their content appears in your Google Reader as it's published.

The trick is to subscribe to as many feeds as you can find in the area of law that you'll be covering. If you're following different categories of topics, you can organize the feeds into groups. Make sure you get a broad cross section of feeds to ensure you keep abreast of important developments and developing consensus.

If you don't like looking at feeds in a browser, you can download a standalone RSS reader that will work as software you run on your computer. The most popular reader for the Mac is NetNewsWire (netnewswireapp. com), which is free with ads, or $14.99 (a one-time payment) if you want the ads removed. The popular option for PCs is FeedDemon (FeedDemon. com), also free, with a premium version that costs a total of $19.99. Both tools synchronize with Google Reader, which is useful if you get to the point where you're reading your feeds across several computers and devices.

Once your RSS reader is set up and synced across all you devices, you should develop a regular reading schedule. Since all RSS readers have an option to flag articles, flag anything you come across that could be fodder for a blog post. The RSS reader will group your flagged posts together so you can easily find them later.

It will take a few weeks to get comfortable using an RSS reader, but once you catch on, you'll appreciate how much easier it is to stay on top of the legal news relevant to your blog.

Blogs

Finding blogs to follow is simply a matter of looking at the various blog directories with which you registered your own blog (see Lesson 7). Even if you are going to try to follow only blogs that are directly related to your topic, I'd still include a few blogs that are general news sources. Take a close look at the blogs that the *ABA Journal* selected as the Top 100 for the past year: abajournal.com/blawg100.

It can't be stressed enough: you want to subscribe to as many blogs as possible. The more you follow, the more interesting content you'll be alerted to, and if you don't like a blog, you can easily unsubscribe later.

Social Media

In addition to an RSS reader for blogs, you should monitor social media services like Twitter, LinkedIn, and perhaps even Facebook. Again, the more news sources you're using to track developments in your topic area, the easier it will be to generate ideas for blog posts. Writing the posts will be easier as well, because you'll have online source material to link to.

Since Twitter has become the premier source for breaking news, you will need to learn to use it as a news-gathering tool. The more people you follow on Twitter, the easier it is to gather news for the blurbs you are posting on Twitter.

TweetDeck and Buffer—the social media services described in Lesson 7—can be used to gather information as well as distribute it. TweetDeck, in particular, is great for following a lot of different Twitter streams because you can filter things easily. For example, if you're waiting for a federal election result, you can construct a search string to pull tweets that discuss when a news organization has called the election for a certain state. The results you get from a Twitter feed will be faster than watching the cable news channels, and if you cross-check Tweets against each other, more reliable.

LinkedIn and Facebook can also be great for mining story ideas, but since a lot of content that appears in your RSS reader and Twitter feed will reappear on LinkedIn and Facebook, monitoring those sources is probably not as important. Google⁺ is also a social media site that many people are starting to use. It's too early to tell if Google⁺ will develop the same traction as Facebook and Twitter, but it certainly can't be completely ignored. If you have a Google account you'll automatically be given a Google⁺ account, so play with it and see if you can make it work for you.

The more channels of communication you can pay attention to, the more content you'll have to select from in crafting content for your blog.

Final Thoughts

Ethical Considerations

Lawyers like to focus on the things that can go wrong before they take action. Here's a short list of possible problems that might arise from posting to a blog:

- Ethics complaint for not complying with applicable advertising restrictions on lawyers
- Ethics trouble for comments that are deemed unprofessional or otherwise improper
- Inadvertent disclosure of client confidences, or waiver of an attorney-client privilege
- Inadvertent creation of an attorney-client relationship
- Inadvertent misrepresentation, often the result of relying on an assistant who is focused on marketing but is unfamiliar with professional responsibility rules.
- A blog post that contradicts a legal or factual position you've taken elsewhere

If your state has rules regarding lawyer advertising, you should become very familiar with them and make sure you avoid violating them.

My general rule for blogging is almost guaranteed to avoid any kind of ethics problem: I don't blog (or say anything at all online) about any client matters with one exception: if a case is truly final, I may briefly comment on the outcome if it's of interest to others. I don't use my blog to overtly self-promote, which avoids having to weigh the applicability of advertising restrictions.

If you're worried about someone reading your blog and thinking you've somehow become his or her lawyer, you can include a disclaimer on your main page. Although I don't post such a disclaimer, many lawyer-bloggers do.

Be careful of unsolicited e-mails asking for specific legal advice; you don't want to leave open an argument that an attorney-client relationship arose. Most of the e-mails you'll get will be from people seeking free advice, including advice about matters in a jurisdiction where you aren't licensed to practice law.

I suggest preparing a form response something like this: "I received your e-mail, and while I would love to help you, I'm not able to accept you as a client. I recommend you contact the local bar association in the state where you live and ask for help finding a suitable attorney to handle your problem." That serves to formally decline representation in writing, but in a way that's not too curt.

The easiest way to get in trouble with your blog is to say something really offensive. Even if it's not an ethical violation, it can still do damage. Avoid posting anything to your blog when you're upset. In fact, make it a rule to never publish a post anything immediately after writing it. Setting all of your posts to go off in the future, per the delayed posting discussion in Lesson 6, will give you time to reflect on what you've written. If you intend to write caustic commentary, which is certainly your First Amendment right, just be aware that the risks of stirring up needless controversy increases. Learn to distinguish between controversy and needless controversy.

Best Tips for Success

If you want to stand out among all the blogs on the Internet, you have to do something that few people are doing. Here's my recommendation: be honest and down-to-earth about what you believe and why you believe it. Don't be quick to condemn other people's beliefs; strive to understand other points of view. Look for common ground and ways to help other bloggers. Write well and post often—and, if you can't post often, then at least post with predictable regularity.

Conclusion

Congratulations on setting up your blog, and good luck! The hardest part is over. And remember, nothing is set in stone: if you need to change the design of your blog you can do so easily, and the change will automatically apply to all posts, even the ones that have been archived.

There's much more to learn about blogging, but the best way to learn is by doing. The book has come to an end, but you can get more information by following the companion blog at onehrblog.com. And if you have questions about anything related to setting up a law blog, feel free to e-mail me at ernie@ernestsvenson.com.

APPENDIX

Recommended Law Blogs

Here are six law-related blogs that you can investigate to get a feel for how different lawyers use their blogs. Notice the varied design styles, frequency of posts, and writing styles. All are engaging in different ways.

Law21.ca

Jordan Furlong's "Law21" blog describes itself as providing "dispatches from a legal profession on the brink." Jordan is a lawyer, speaker, and consultant based in Ottawa, Canada. His passion is explaining how technology is pressuring changes in the legal profession. Jordan is an excellent writer, and his posts are always a model of deferential thoughtfulness. If you can emulate Jordan's engaging style, you'll have captured something valuable. His posts are longer than most blog posts, which is suits the topics he addresses, but the length also requires extra diligence. He uses WordPress as his blogging software.

DennisKennedy.com/blog

Dennis also writes about technology. His posts are short and sweet, and he tends to discuss new software tools and mobile applications and how they might be useful to lawyers. Note that Dennis's blog is embedded into his website; this is an option, but it's not always easy to achieve unless you plan for it from the start or engage a savvy web consultant.

BowTielaw.wordpress.com

Josh Gilliland's site is "dedicated to untying the knotty issues of e-Discovery," but it also gets its name from the fact that Josh likes to wear bow ties. You'll note that the word *wordpress* is in the URL name, which means his blog is hosted by WordPress. His blog is focused on a niche area: e-Discovery. Josh doesn't try to cover all of the latest breaking news in the world of e-Discovery; he selects key cases and dissects them carefully, and he finishes by offering the key takeaway from the case. Also worth noting is that Josh uses images in his posts, usually several per post. This helps break up the monotony of solid text.

AbnormalUse.com

This blog is managed by Jim Dedman, an attorney with a 50-lawyer firm based in South Carolina. Several lawyers in the firm assist Jim. The blog focuses on product liability litigation in state and federal court, and the topics are presented in clever ways that engage readers. The site has twice been honored as a Top 100 Blog by the *ABA Journal* in the category of torts, and with good reason: it shows that a group of lawyers can create a really clever blog with lots of personality.

NOLACriminalLaw.com

Townsend Myers is a solo criminal defense attorney in New Orleans and does mostly state court work. His website has an embedded blog, which is built on the WordPress platform. Townsend writes infrequently but effectively. He covers topics like underage drinking and drug use, which are written as informative commentary, but also contain keywords likely to show up in a web search. He reports that his blog has been very useful in getting new business and doesn't take up much time. He also uses Twitter to complement his blogging efforts.

employeeatty.blogspot.com

This employment law blog is actually titled "Screw You Guys, I'm Going Home," but that's not the domain name (perhaps it was already taken). Written by Donna Ballman, a lawyer in Florida, this blog is notable for a couple of reasons: First, it's hosted on Blogger, which is the free blogging platform operated by Google. Second, Ms. Ballman offers employment law tips at the end of most posts. Many attorneys would be hesitant to do this, but done properly—as Ms. Ballman does—it's a great way to establish your deep knowledge in a subject area. Notice that her site incorporates the latest tweets from her Twitter page, which is a common setup. This blog was also nominated as a Top 100 Blog by the *ABA Journal*.

Recommended Reading

Below are some blog articles and books that can help you learn how to write crisply, and strategically build an audience.

Ahmed, Safeer, "How To Register Your Blog In Technorati?," http://www.howdoblog.com/2012/04/how-to-register-your-blog-in-technorati.html

American Bar Association, "ABA Commission on Ethics 20/20," http://www.americanbar.org/groups/professional_responsibility/aba_commission_on_ethics_20_20.html

American Bar Association, "ABA Formal Opinion 10-457, Lawyer Websites," (August 2010), http://www.americanbar.org/content/dam/aba/migrated/cpr/pdfs/10_457.authcheckdam.pdf

American Bar Association, "ABA Model Rules of Professional Conduct," http://www.americanbar.org/groups/professional_responsibility/publications/model_rules_of_professional_conduct/model_rules_of_professional_conduct_table_of_contents.html

Beck, James, "On Self Promotion," http://druganddevicelaw.blogspot.com/2011/12/on-self-promotion.html

Blogger Central, "25 Quick SEO Tips And Tricks To Start Your Blog," http://www.bloggersentral.com/2012/04/25-quick-seo-tricks-to-start-your-blog.html

Carnegie, Dale, *How to Win Friends and Influence People* (Simon and Schuster, 1936)

Clark, Roy Peter, *Writing Tools: 50 Essential Strategies for Every Writer* (Little, Brown and Company, 2006)

Dedman, Jim, "How To Blog: A Primer (And Not A Boring Primer Either)," http://www.nclawblog.com/journal/2012/3/14/how-to-blog-a-primer-and-not-a-boring-primer-either.html

Elefant, Carolyn and Nicole Black, *Social Media for Lawyers: The Next Frontier* (American Bar Association, 2010)

Fish, Stanley, *How to Write a Sentence—And How to Read One* (HarperCollins, 2011)

Goding, Seth, *Permission Marketing: Turning Strangers Into Friends And Friends Into Customers* (Simon and Schuster, 1999)

Golden, Michelle, *Social Media Strategies for Professionals and Their Firms: The Guide to Establishing Credibility and Accelerating Relationships*, (Wiley Professional Advisory, 2010)

Greenfield, Scott H., "Why Bother?" http://blog.simplejustice.us/2011/12/08/why-bother.aspx

Hyatt, Michael, "How to Launch a Self-Hosted WordPress Blog in 20 Minutes or Less," http://michaelhyatt.com/ez-wordpress-setup.html

Jaksch, Mary, "The New Style of Writing for the Net (Are You Up with the Play?)," http://writetodone.com/2012/05/14/new-style-blog-writing/

Kennedy, Dennis, and Allison Shields, *LinkedIn In in One Hour For Lawyers* (American Bar Association, 2012)

Lantz, Jeff, *Internet Branding for Lawyers: Building the Client-Centered Website* (American Bar Association, 2012)

Levine, Rick and Doc Searls, David Weinberger, Christopher Locke, *The Cluetrain Manifesto* (Perseus Publishing, 2000)

Levitt, Carole and Mark Rosch, *The Cybersleuth's Guide to the Internet: Conducting Effective Free Investigative and Legal Research on the Web* (American Bar Association, 2012)

McDonough, Molly, "To Ernie Svenson, Blogging is 'Largely a Selfish Activity,' " http://www.abajournal.com/magazine/article/to_ernie_svenson_blogging_is_largely_a_selfish_activity/

Mighell, Tom, "The Next Stage of Lawyer Blogging," *Law Practice Magazine* (American Bar Association Law Practice Management Section, April/May 2006), http://www.americanbar.org/publications/law_practice_home/law_practice_archive/lpm_magazine_articles_v32_is3_an2.html

O'Keefe, Kevin, "4 in 10 Law Firms Report Landing New Clients Through Blogging And Other Social Media," http://kevin.lexblog.com/2012/02/29/4-in-10-law-firms-report-landing-new-clients-through-blogging-and-other-social-media/

O'Keefe, Kevin, "15 Questions On Blogging and Social Media for Lawyers, Interview with Business Journal," http://kevin.lexblog.com/2012/03/08/15-questions-on-blogging-and-social-media-for-lawyers-interview-with-business-journal/

O'Keefe, Kevin, "Blogging and Social Media as Learning Tools for Lawyers," http://kevin.lexblog.com/2012/06/05/blogging-and-social-media-as-learning-tools-for-lawyers/

O'Reilly, Tim and Sarah Milstein, *The Twitter Book* (O'Reilly, 2012)

Orwell, George, "Politics and the English Language," http://www.orwell.ru/essays/politics/english/e_polit

Poje, Joshua, J.D., "Legal Ethics and Policy Considerations in E-Communications and Social Media," (ABA Legal Technology Resource Center), http://www.iml.org/files/pages/4213/LegalEthicsSocialMedia.pdf

Svenson, Ernest, "Building A Better Blog," http://www.americanbar.org/publications/law_practice_magazine/2012/january_february/building-a-better-blog.html

Trunk, Penelope, "Penelope's Guide to Blogging," http://blog.penelopetrunk.com/penelopes-guide-to-blogging/

Checklist For New Bloggers

Here's a useful checklist of common tasks related to blogging. Most of it comes from the things we've talked about in the book. Keep it handy as you set up your blog and start posting to it.

Before You Do Anything

- ☐ Review ABA Model Rule 7.1 and any corresponding rule in your jurisdiction.
- ☐ Review ABA Formal Opinion 10-457 and any corresponding rule in your jurisdiction.
- ☐ Research local ethics rules regarding advertising and online publishing.

Before You Decide on a Blog Topic

- ☐ List three goals for blog in order of priority.
- ☐ List main topics for blog.

☐ Start brainstorming the name of your blog, and look for domain names that correspond to it. Go to <u>bustaname.com</u> to help you come up with ideas.

☐ Write a short blurb describing what your blog is about; this will be used as an "About This Blog" page later.

Preparing to Set Up a Blog

☐ Register the domain name that you like as soon as you settle on it; if you're torn between two or three grab them all. You can release the rejects once you make up your mind.

☐ Setup a Twitter account with a name similar to your blog's name.

☐ After you zero in on a topic and a name, locate similar law-related blogs and study their posts. Note whether they have comments, how long the posts are, the number of authors who contribute, whether they have images, and so on.

☐ Visit the ABA directory of law blogs and examine several to get a feel for the different types of blogs used by lawyers and to get a sense of as many different approaches as possible.

☐ Make a short list of three or four of the blogs you most admire and see if you can get in touch with the authors by e-mail. Ask them questions like the ones listed at the end of Lesson 1.

☐ Identify law bloggers in your city and invite them to lunch to pick their brains. (If there are none in your city, visit the ABA TECH-SHOW in Chicago, which is held in late March each year; you'll find plenty of well-known law bloggers there at the "Beer for Bloggers" event that is usually sponsored by LexBlog's Kevin O'Keefe).

☐ Decide how much design work you want for your blog. At a minimum choose something clean and easy to navigate; you can change it later if you want. But if you want something spectacular, then you should make finding a good designer a top priority.

☐ Decide on a blogging platform (e.g., WordPress, TypePad, etc.) and determine whether you're going to try to set it up yourself or whether you need help.

☐ If you need help, locate someone who can help you set up and design your blog. TypePad offers this service for $349, and you'd be well advised to take advantage of it if you want a TypePad blog.

☐ If you're setting up a WordPress blog and need help, check out oDesk.com, which is the best place to get low-cost help for web-related tasks.

☐ Set up an RSS reader and subscribe to all of the law blogs and sources that cover topics similar to yours. (You can find them through the ABA Blawg Directory.)

☐ Find out if those blogs have Twitter feeds and investigate the feeds to figure out if you want to follow them—later.

☐ Don't follow anyone on Twitter until you start posting; as you follow folks they'll check you out and might follow you back. If you have a blog, they might start following it in their RSS reader; if you don't, they won't. So wait to follow on Twitter until your blog goes live.

☐ Set up an account with Feedblitz so that people can subscribe to your blog by e-mail. You want to capture e-mail addresses, and this is the best way to do. Besides, lots of people prefer to follow blogs by e-mail versus RSS readers.

☐ Set up a Feedburner account so you can monitor the number of people that subscribe to your blog, and get other detailed statistics.

☐ Decide what categories you'll be using for your posts, if any. Remember, you don't want too many. You can always add more if you need to.

☐ Make sure to set up an "About This Blog" page based on what you wrote up as a result of an earlier checklist item. (Include author bios for all the contributing members of the blog.)

☐ Create a short disclaimer for your blog along the lines discussed in the "Final Thoughts" section.

After Set Up but before You Launch Your Site

☐ Before you start posting, spend a few weeks coming up with posts on topics that aren't time-sensitive. Have them ready to go, but don't release them too quickly. These will serve as a buffer for when you get too busy to post regularly.

☐ After you have several posts up, start following people on Twitter and using Twitter to let people know you're blogging.

☐ The way to alert people on Twitter is to link to lots of interesting stuff and then weave in periodic links to your posts.

☐ Don't ask people to follow you or to follow your blog; that doesn't work. Be cheerful, helpful, and informative.

☐ Register your blog with the services listed in Lesson 7.

☐ Remember to link to other bloggers often. Use links in your posts as much as possible.

☐ Use links to refer to things that are defined or explained elsewhere. In short, learn all the ways of linking.

☐ For a master course in hyperlinking that's compressed into one blog post, closely study Jordan Furlong's "Law School Revolution" (http://www.law21.ca/2012/06/25/law-school-revolution/).

☐ Buy the book *LinkedIn in One Hour for Lawyers* by Dennis Kennedy and Allison Shields and implement the strategies discussed there to build the audience for your blog and your law practice in general.

☐ Buy and read Dale Carnegie's *How to Win Friends and Influence People*, and make notes on how those principles can be used to build an audience for your blog.

☐ Subscribe to Seth Godin's blog in your RSS reader, and also subscribe to his daily e-mail. Follow his advice closely. No one alive today better understands how to make use of the Internet to build a strong audience of loyal followers.

☐ Update your blog frequently, and on as regular a schedule as possible.

☐ As you draft your posts always keep in mind George Orwell's six rules for effective writing: (1) never use a metaphor, simile, or other figure of speech which you are used to seeing in print; (2) never use a long word where a short one will do; (3) if it is possible to cut a word out, always cut it out; (4) never use the passive where you can use the active; (5) never use a foreign phrase, a scientific word, or a jargon word if you can think of an everyday English equivalent; (6) break any of these rules sooner than say anything outright barbarous.

Creating Posts: Basic Checklist

☐ Make sure you're in the Rich Text view, and not HTML view.

☐ Draft the post and apply basic formatting.

☐ Run spell check.

☐ Enter keywords and Technorati tags if you want.

☐ Set comments on, or off, as you prefer.

☐ Set publication time and date if you want the post to go off in the future.

☐ Click the Preview button to see what post will look like when published; check all hyperlinks for validity.

☐ If everything is in order, click the Publish button.

Index

SELECTED BOOKS FROM

iPad in One Hour for Lawyers, Second Edition
By Tom Mighell

Product Code: 5110747 / LPM Price: $24.95 / Regular Price: $39.95

Whether you are a new or a more advanced iPad user, *iPad in One Hour for Lawyers* takes a great deal of the mystery and confusion out of using your iPad. Ideal for lawyers who want to get up to speed swiftly, this book presents the essentials so you don't get bogged down in technical jargon and extraneous features and apps. In just six, short lessons, you'll learn how to:

- Quickly Navigate and Use the iPad User Interface
- Set Up Mail, Calendar, and Contacts
- Create and Use Folders to Multitask and Manage Apps
- Add Files to Your iPad, and Sync Them
- View and Manage Pleadings, Case Law, Contracts, and other Legal Documents
- Use Your iPad to Take Notes and Create Documents
- Use Legal-Specific Apps at Trial or in Doing Research

Google for Lawyers: Essential Search Tips and Productivity Tools
By Carole A. Levitt and Mark E. Rosch

Product Code: 5110704 / LPM Price: $47.95 / Regular Price: $79.95

This book introduces novice Internet searchers to the diverse collection of information locatable through Google. The book discusses the importance of including effective Google searching as part of a lawyer's due diligence, and cites case law that mandates that lawyers should use Google and other resources available on the Internet, where applicable. For intermediate and advanced users, the book unlocks the power of various advanced search strategies and hidden search features they might not be aware of.

iPad Apps in One Hour for Lawyers
By Tom Mighell

Product Code: 5110739 / LPM Price: $19.95 / Regular Price: $34.95

At last count, there were more than 80,000 apps available for the iPad. Finding the best apps often can be an overwhelming, confusing, and frustrating process. iPad Apps in One Hour for Lawyers provides the "best of the best" apps that are essential for any law practice. In just one hour, you will learn about the apps most worthy of your time and attention. This book will describe how to buy, install, and update iPad apps, and help you:

- Find apps to get organized and improve your productivity
- Create, manage, and store documents on your iPad
- Choose the best apps for your law office, including litigation and billing apps
- Find the best news, reading, and reference apps
- Take your iPad on the road with apps for travelers
- Maximize your social networking power
- Have some fun with game and entertainment apps during your relaxation time

The Electronic Evidence and Discovery Handbook: Forms, Checklists, and Guidelines
By Sharon D. Nelson, Bruce A. Olson, and John W. Simek

Product Code: 5110569 / LPM Price: $99.95 / Regular Price: $129.95

The use of electronic evidence has increased dramatically over the past few years, but many lawyers still struggle with the complexities of electronic discovery. This substantial book provides lawyers with the templates they need to frame their discovery requests and provides helpful advice on what they can subpoena. In addition to the ready-made forms, the authors also supply explanations to bring you up to speed on the electronic discovery field. The accompanying CD-ROM features over 70 forms, including, Motions for Protective Orders, Preservation and Spoliation Documents, Motions to Compel, Electronic Evidence Protocol Agreements, Requests for Production, Internet Services Agreements, and more. Also included is a full electronic evidence case digest with over 300 cases detailed!

The Lawyer's Guide to Microsoft Word 2010
By Ben M. Schorr

Product Code: 5110721 / LPM Price: $41.95 / Regular Price: $69.95

Microsoft® Word is one of the most used applications in the Microsoft® Office suite. This handy reference includes clear explanations, legal-specific descriptions, and time-saving tips for getting the most out of Microsoft Word®—and customizing it for the needs of today's legal professional. Focusing on the tools and features that are essential for lawyers in their everyday practice, this book explains in detail the key components to help make you more effective, more efficient, and more successful.

LinkedIn in One Hour for Lawyers
By Dennis Kennedy and Allison C. Shields

Product Code: 5110737 / LPM Price: $19.95 / Regular Price: $34.95

Lawyers work in a world of networks, connections, referrals, and recommendations. For many lawyers, the success of these networks determines the success of their practice. LinkedIn®, the premier social networking tool for business, can help you create, nurture, and expand your professional network and gain clients in the process. LinkedIn® in One Hour for Lawyers provides an introduction to this powerful tool in terms that any attorney can understand. In just one hour, you will learn to:

- Set up a LinkedIn account
- Complete your basic profile
- Create a robust, dynamic profile that will attract clients
- Build your connections
- Use search tools to enhance your network
- Maximize your presence with features such as groups, updates, answers, and recommendations
- Monitor your network with ease
- Optimize your settings for privacy concerns
- Use LinkedIn® effectively in the hiring process
- Develop a LinkedIn strategy to grow your legal network

SELECTED BOOKS FROM

Virtual Law Practice:
How to Deliver Legal Services Online
By Stephanie L. Kimbro

Product Code: 5110707 / LPM Price: $47.95 / Regular Price: $79.95

The legal market has recently experienced a dramatic shift as lawyers seek out alternative methods of practicing law and providing more affordable legal services. Virtual law practice is revolutionizing the way the public receives legal services and how legal professionals work with clients. If you are interested in this form of practicing law, *Virtual Law Practice* will help you:

- *Responsibly deliver legal services online to* your clients
- Successfully set up and operate a virtual law office
- Establish a virtual law practice online through a secure, client-specific portal
- Manage and market your virtual law practice
- Understand state ethics and advisory opinions
- Find more flexibility and work/life balance in the legal profession

The Lawyer's Essential Guide to Writing
By Marie Buckley

Product Code: 5110726 / LPM Price: $47.95 / Regular Price: $79.95

This is a readable, concrete guide to contemporary legal writing. Based on Marie Buckley's years of experience coaching lawyers, this book provides a systematic approach to all forms of written communication, from memoranda and briefs to e-mail and blogs. The book sets forth three principles for powerful writing and shows how to apply those principles to develop a clean and confident style.

Find Info Like a Pro, Volume 1: Mining the Internet's Publicly Available Resources for Investigative Research
By Carole A. Levitt and Mark E. Rosch

Product Code: 5110708 / LPM Price: $47.95 / Regular Price: $79.95

This complete hands-on guide shares the secrets, shortcuts, and realities of conducting investigative and background research using the sources of publicly available information available on the Internet. Written for legal professionals, this comprehensive desk book lists, categorizes, and describes hundreds of free and fee-based Internet sites. The resources and techniques in this book are useful for investigations; depositions; locating missing witnesses, clients, or heirs; and trial preparation, among other research challenges facing legal professionals. In addition, a CD-ROM is included, which features clickable links to all of the sites contained in the book.

How to Start and Build a Law Practice, Platinum Fifth Edition
By Jay G Foonberg

Product Code: 5110508 / LPM Price: $57.95 / Regular Price: $69.95

This classic ABA bestseller has been used by tens of thousands of lawyers as the comprehensive guide to planning, launching, and growing a successful practice. It's packed with over 600 pages of guidance on identifying the right location, finding clients, setting fees, managing your office, maintaining an ethical and responsible practice, maximizing available resources, upholding your standards, and much more. You'll find the information you need to successfully launch your practice, run it at maximum efficiency, and avoid potential pitfalls along the way. If you're committed to starting—and growing—your own practice, this one book will give you the expert advice you need to make it succeed for years to come.

Microsoft OneNote in One Hour for Lawyers
By Ben M. Schorr

Product Code: 5110731 / LPM Price: $19.95 / Regular Price: $34.95

Each copy of Microsoft® Office 2010 sold now includes OneNote, and its usage among lawyers is poised to skyrocket. With this guide, learn to use OneNote in your law practice to save time and increase productivity. Microsoft® OneNote in One Hour for Lawyers will explain, in plain English, how to get started with the software, develop best practices, and become far more effective in your note-taking and research. In just six, short lessons, you will learn how to:

- Get started with your first notebook
- Take notes more effectively
- Add audio and video recordings to notes
- Capture and organize side notes
- Collect research quickly and easily
- Create templates for frequently used notes
- Search and share notebooks
- Integrate OneNote with other applications such as Microsoft® Outlook and Microsoft® Word

Social Media for Lawyers: The Next Frontier
By Carolyn Elefant and Nicole Black

Product Code: 5110710 / LPM Price: $47.95 / Regular Price: $79.95

The world of legal marketing has changed with the rise of social media sites such as Linkedin, Twitter, and Facebook. Law firms are seeking their companies attention with tweets, videos, blog posts, pictures, and online content. Social media is fast and delivers news at record pace. This book provides you with a practical, goal-centric approach to using social media in your law practice that will enable you to identify social media platforms and tools that fit your practice and implement them easily, efficiently, and ethically.

30-DAY RISK-FREE ORDER FORM

ABA **LawPracticeManagementSection**
MARKETING • MANAGEMENT • TECHNOLOGY • FINANCE

Please print or type. To ship UPS, we must have your street address. If you list a P.O. Box, we will ship by U.S. Mail.

Name

Member ID

Firm/Organization

Street Address

City/State/Zip

Area Code/Phone (In case we have a question about your order)

E-mail

Method of Payment:
❑ Check enclosed, payable to American Bar Association
❑ MasterCard ❑ Visa ❑ American Express

Card Number   Expiration Date

Signature Required

MAIL THIS FORM TO:
American Bar Association, Publication Orders
P.O. Box 10892, Chicago, IL 60610

ORDER BY PHONE:
24 hours a day, 7 days a week:
Call 1-800-285-2221 to place a credit card order.
We accept Visa, MasterCard, and American Express.

EMAIL ORDERS: orders@americanbar.org
FAX: 1-312-988-5568

VISIT OUR WEB SITE: www.ShopABA.org
Allow 7-10 days for regular UPS delivery. Need it sooner? Ask about our overnight delivery options. Call the ABA Service Center at 1-800-285-2221 for more information.

GUARANTEE:
If—for any reason—you are not satisfied with your purchase, you may return it within 30 days of receipt for a refund of the price of the book(s). No questions asked.

Thank You For Your Order.

Join the ABA Law Practice Management Section today and receive a substantial discount on Section publications!

Product Code:	Description:	Quantity:	Price:	Total Price:
				$
				$
				$
				$
				$

**Shipping/Handling:		***Tax:**		
$0.00 to $9.99	add $0.00	IL residents add 9.5%	Subtotal:	$
$10.00 to $49.99	add $5.95	DC residents add 6%	*Tax:	$
$50.00 to $99.99	add $7.95		**Shipping/Handling:	$
$100.00 to $199.99	add $9.95	Yes, I am an ABA member and would like to join the Law Practice Management Section today! (Add $50.00)		$
$200.00 to $499.99	add $12.95		Total:	$